Chainsaw Chronicles

Reflections of a Chainsaw Sculptor

Joe King

Dear Carole,

To my newest "Unique Trees"
Brother in Arms, it's been
great fun getting to know you,
And I look forward to many
years of new friendship!

Thank you, stay healthy and
wish you all the best!

xo - your new buddy Joe :)

For Jasmine and Bailey,

Some things I didn't have a chance to tell you…

.

Prologue

"Friends are an oasis in human relationships."

I've heard it said that "we become what we are," and I believe this is true. In more simple terms, we've all heard the saying "crabby old man," and this is only a half-truth. A more accurate way to phrase it would be: "he's a crabby man and now he's old." "Such a kind old lady," is the same thing; she's a kind lady and now she's old (older). We become what we are.

People come into our lives at random times and help change or shape us in some small way, often times without knowing, and help us become what we are. I mention a few of them in this memoir, but leave out so many others. Each and every one are no less important to the person I have become and the stories that follow. If you find your name here without acknowledgment or prior permission, or don't find yourself among my important life moments that I recount, please accept my thanks and apologies in advance. Writing one's life story is a daunting endeavor, and just know that I will always be thankful for our friendship.

CONTENTS

One

Cheboksary ...

I felt the soft, steady, clickety-clack rhythm of the rails begin to slow a bit, which signaled our approach to Kanash Station, the only noteworthy stop on an overnight train ride from Moscow to Cheboksary. In this station, one had just enough time to step off the train for a smoke, stretch the legs, or find something to eat from one of the ever-present local vendors who populate most train and bus stations. Traditional air-dried and heavily salted fish was a popular item, and lots of people grabbed some to take home so as not to show up empty-handed, I suppose. But it must be an acquired taste: smelly stuff wrapped in old newspaper and shoved under a bunk, which you were then able to "enjoy" for the remainder of the trip.

That aside, you always meet interesting people along the way, and this particular time it started out with our cabin attendant, the *Provodnitsa*. Short, dark hair, squeaky little voice in a crisp, sharply pressed uniform, absolutely no sense of humor, and a perky balance to her step that could only have come from many years navigating a bumpy, swerving hallway. This particular lady was very animated and I remember thinking she could easily find work in Disneyland if only she could learn to smile a bit more. Keep in mind, it was quite different from Russian airlines where most attendants knew a little English; on the trains, I hadn't met one yet. On her first round to inspect our tickets and passports, she made a point to glare at our two male cabin mates, then growled, "And don't get this American drunk, he might start some trouble." Maybe she'd had some bad experiences in the past, but those guys didn't listen anyhow, they never did. Ten seconds later, out came the snacks, a bottle of vodka, some stinky fish, and another memorable train ride.

Overnight traveling by train was a breeze compared to the long overseas flights. Whether out of nervousness or just plain discomfort from being cramped up with a bunch of strangers, it was nearly impossible to sleep. That was never a problem on domestic flights where sometimes I could be asleep before the plane got off the ground, but not international flights; it was just too exciting to even think about sleeping. It could also stretch into two sleepless nights, which included getting excited the night before the beginning of a big new adventure, especially if it happened to be somewhere really interesting or different. Say, for example, a trip to the motherland. What follows here is a story written for my wood carving magazine over ten years ago, and I've copied it here.

{Begin article}

I grew up during our cold war period with the Soviet Union, and although very young at the time, I clearly remember not only the political tensions, but also the great mysteries surrounding this enormous 'empire' on the other side of the world. In fact, many books and journals from others traveling to Russia begin with a similar theme: an early fascination coupled with a nagging curiosity to see what those people were really like. There were so many stereotypes floating around back then, like James Bond spy movies that left us with absolutely no doubt who the bad guys were. But every once in a while you would see a famous composer, or a candid family photo and think, "Hey, they look just like us!"

This story begins on my second trip to Russia. The year was 2009, almost two decades after the Berlin Wall came down and subsequent breakup of the communist Soviet Union. The year before I had met a Russian girl in Spain, it was starting to get serious and the term 'long-distance relationship' was taken to a whole new level.

From door to door it was almost six thousand miles with several connections, including the ten-hour flight to Moscow, an overnight sleeper car train ride, and a handful of taxi rides. Finally I arrived two days later in central Russia, and her home city of Cheboksary, in the region of the Chuvashia Republic, a place that possibly more than any other portrays the old-world colorful and artistically designed costumes you might see in a travel magazine. Oftentimes the famous 'Matryoshka dolls' (small, wooden nesting dolls, often bought as souvenirs, where one is stacked inside another) were painted in the brightly colored costume garb you'd see at almost every celebration.

Cheboksary is a middle-sized city, roughly the size of my hometown of Pittsburgh, with just under half a million people. The city center is perched directly on the famous Volga, the longest river in Europe and almost a mile wide at that point on its twenty-two-hundred-mile journey to the Caspian Sea. In typical European style, the public transportation system was extremely efficient and it was possible to travel almost anywhere by trolley bus for eleven rubles (fifteen cents at the time).

Moving away from the modern city center, I found the many sprawling high-rise "flats," which were almost like little communities within themselves. Oftentimes they're built in a circular fashion with room for a good-size playground area, a bit of parking, and a "magazine" (small convenience store) by each different entrance. From the outside it had kind of a sterile turn-of-the-century look, but inside, and regardless of the age or configuration, they were all warm and cozy. Very warm in fact; the central heating system piped hot water throughout during the winter months and sometimes the only way to turn it down was to open a window.

Moving still farther out, I found myself in connecting villages, remnants of the old-world Russian life with little wooden houses that all had a garden and various livestock milling around, mostly unfenced. There you could also start to find the family "dachas," or modest summer homes, which were sometimes grouped together and somewhat similar to an RV park in the states, also with a garden. I should also mention that most of Russia lies in northern regions and enjoys extended daylight hours during the short summers, and subsequently extra-long nights for the better part of the year. It was interesting to discover how their garden vegetables had genetically adapted to a shorter growing season and were extremely hardy.

This particular visit was especially exciting as we had been communicating with city officials for several months about carving a big tree in one of the parks there. Like a normal carving job at home, they sent me photos ahead of time that I was able to study, and then I sent back some ideas of what was possible. It was decided I would create a bear family, which, like many other families from the area, were simply out enjoying a day in the park. Prior to arriving I had shipped a small detail saw over and made arrangements to borrow some other equipment along the way, plus a list of the necessary amount of scaffolding. At home this type of job would normally have taken around two days, but I correctly assumed it might take much longer—almost a full week as it turned out.

The place they selected to do the carving was on the outskirts of town and known as the "Cheboksary Park of 500 Years." As promised, scaffolding was provided but it was very old and primitive and turned out to be a creative adventure of its own. The good news, however, was that all of the chainsaws they provided for me were modern, brand new Husqvarna's, and they also offered just about anything else I needed.

One of the chainsaw stores was located across town in the new 'Mega Mall,' and what a strange experience it was to walk through a modern mall wielding chainsaws, but nobody there gave it a second glance. Equipment logistics actually included three stops: saws from one place, bar & chain oil from another, then a third stop for 'benzene' at a local filling station.

The morning bus ride to the park was always an adventure. No matter how hard I tried to blend in, it was never possible, partly due to the fact I was always loaded down with a heavy backpack and huge equipment bag. Possibly also due to the fact that I didn't look or dress like a Russian. Whenever possible I would try to find a window seat for the twenty-minute or so ride to the park so I could photograph some of the wonderful early summer fruit trees that were all in full bloom at this time. Plus a window seat would allow me to be a bit less noticeable. You were hard-pressed to take a bad picture in any direction.

One morning while snapping away, my wallet fell out and onto the seat without my noticing. This is considered a cardinal sin there, anywhere actually, and it was the first time it had ever happened in my life. As luck would have it, there was an elderly Babushka sitting beside me. She happened to see it fall and, man, did I ever get chewed out. She had a mixed look of bewilderment, disbelief, and curiosity, and eventually I came to realize it was the same everywhere with preconceived notions. Just as I used James Bond movies as an example, many Russians, I suppose, saw American television and thought we were all like that. For example, the Disney Channel was very popular there, and on that channel, the families were rich, the kids spoiled, and the parents all stupid. Need I say more? This, however, became one of the more interesting aspects of the entire trip as I was the first "real American" many of the people in the region had ever met in person.

Arriving at the park, I came to realize it was much bigger than I had anticipated and a very popular destination with quite a variety of attractions. They also had a very smart and funny director, Igor (whom I have since become good friends with), along with his secretary, Yula, who could easily place in any beauty contest. I need to interrupt for a moment here to expand on this subject. There are beautiful women all over the world, and I soon came to realize that Russia is where they grow them. Everywhere I turned, I found them in abundance in all age, shapes and sizes, and many is the time I looked around at a bus stop and wondered if the Miss Universe pageant was in town. Of this I am not at all exaggerating in the least. Russian women love their high heels and always on the cutting edge of fashion. For example, one year I noticed a lot of tight, black leather pants, then within a very short time it would became popular in the rest of Europe before eventually making its way across the Atlantic to America. Anyway, back to the park now.

In the main office, they had a German Shepherd guard dog named Bob, or "Booba," whom I also became friends with and soon discovered that most Russian dogs had American names. Working outside on the project I had two helpers when needed, and a translator was available on occasion, but most of the time we managed by using hand signals and the occasional pantomime. By the end of the week, most of the carving was finished and two days of dedication ceremonies were scheduled. This included a speech by the mayor of Cheboksary, various groups of young musicians from the local culture center, sponsors, groups of other children bused in for day-long field trips, as well as art students from the university. Each day also included various public media interviews, newspaper reporters, magazine writers, and television personalities, all who came to see the "famous American artist." I can truthfully say it was one of the most interesting and moving events of my life.

Part of the dedication also included the making up and telling of a story behind the carving: "Bears have picnic in the park." It was pretty straightforward: Bear cubs just goofing around and climbing the tree like normal cubs do. Standing watch beside them was concerned Papa Bear looking after them. "*Austa rōshna*," he warned (be careful), and Mama Bear with lunch ready—a big pot of honey, of course. The best part was a small bunny rabbit and butterfly I made near the base, and as the story goes: if you make a wish while rubbing the bunny, it may come true. There were around two hundred kids listening and you could have heard a pin drop at this point. My translator saved the "rub the bunny" part for last, paused for effect, then said, "And who will be first?" Two hundred little hands shot up into the air like lightning!

To experience such a different culture up close and personal was truly the experience of a lifetime, and I wanted more. I found the Russian people to be as warm, friendly, and hospitable as any place I'd ever been, and possibly even more so. Almost everywhere I went they were as interested in meeting me as I was them, and because of that I quite often enjoyed somewhat of a celebrity status. Sitting in an open riverfront café one warm summer evening with some friends, listening to old traditional Russian music softly playing in the background, I wished that everyone back home in America could be as lucky as I was in that moment.

Chainsaw carving was a relatively new form of carving in Russia, but already way more popular than I was initially aware of. On subsequent visits I was involved in various other carving festivals of which I'll write more about later. A little other side note to this opening story, you may ask: What is any great adventure without a little romance? Well, if you remember the girl I met in Spain, where this all started, her name is Nelli and we've recently celebrated our second wedding anniversary.
{End of article}

With my great grandparents in 1957. They were Polish immigrants and owned a tavern in the south-side of Pittsburgh dating back to the 'Great Depression.'

Two

Observatory Hill …

I'd love to start out here by saying what a fun and normal childhood I had growing up in our little suburban town of Manor, but that was not really the case. It wasn't exactly terrible and could be fun at times, but "normal" is a pretty big stretch by any measure. Most of our parents worked back then, mom and dad both, and we were well provided for but left to our own devices for much of the time, so yes, we did get into some things we weren't supposed to. They say we're all a product of our own environment and thank God I was spared from that scenario.

Our town, like so many others around us, had done well in the latter years of the post-war industrial revolution, but gradually slipped away to a somewhat limp economy, and for young people, it started to feel like just a good place to be from. Certain kids were destined for college, but most would end up in trade schools (if lucky), or working for life at the first good job that came along, and thankfully I was spared from that destiny as well. There was also a dark side of town. Bullying was still in fashion and for every bully there were at least one or two assistant bullies, aspiring bullies, and the occasional semi-reformed bully, all going after anybody who seemed different. Scrawny little redhead kids like me tried to stay invisible, but every once in a while we'd end up getting knocked around a bit.

Plus it was rife with all sorts of racial overtones, but thankfully none of that ever stuck; from an early age and throughout the rest of my life, I've always had great interest in meeting anybody who was different than me.

The little schoolhouse we attended was a three-story red brick building and included all twelve grade levels, but this eventually changed as population needs increased and more schools were added, so by my seventh year we were all moved to the fancy new middle school. I can, however, so clearly remember the beginning when all of the big kids were mixed in with us little ones, a last vestige of a bygone era. I can hardly imagine any other place in the world that can stir up memories so quickly, despite the years since I last visited. I have been an extremely avid reader throughout my life and that was where it started. We were all incredibly bored with schoolwork back then and staring out the window wasn't permitted, so I devised another plan; I would hold my subject book upright in front of me during class and place another (smaller) book inside to read. The books included detective novels, sailing adventures, and just about anything I could get my hands on. While the teacher was going through our lessons in front of the room, I was somewhere in the bowels of a great mystery, about to be swallowed up by an unexpected typhoon in the tropics, or freezing to death on some remote and unknown mountain top. It was all pretty clever for someone still in grade school, however, in retrospect I don't think my teachers were fooled for one minute by this ruse and simply accepted it as a reasonable alternative for my type of student.

Over the years I burned through shelf after shelf of old classic books from the school library until that was exhausted, then became a fixture at our local public library as well.

After school, time was mostly spent hanging around with the Morgan Boys, three brothers around the same age who lived a few doors up. The oldest one, 'Bugsy,' was my best friend and somewhat of a role model at the time. He was a physical fitness fanatic and whether by exercising, climbing trees (or buildings), or taking extremely long hikes, he was always challenging us to be stronger and go farther in everything we did. (in later years he would go on to regional boxing tournaments and in the US Marine Corp as well) Plus we lived on the very top of Observatory Hill which had a long, steep street that we would hike up and down several times a day and become a very hearty bunch of lads at a very early age.

One unfortunate thing happened around this time; a trashy new television series called *It Takes a Thief* started where each week they would illustrate different ways to break into buildings without getting caught. As a result we too became proficient in, however before you get the wrong idea I need to point out that we were not stealing anything, just finding ways to get in without getting caught. Most of the time we would hang around for a little while and explore, then back our way out and nobody was ever the wiser. From this garbage TV show we also mastered the fine art of shoplifting as well, but thankfully that was short-lived as the local store owners were such sweet and kind people that one by one, as we all got caught, they would gently shame us into not trying that anymore.

I think what spared me from getting locked into some of the traditional small-town outcomes was spending summers at my grandmother's farm. In the early teen years, we had full access to various adult activities like riding tractors, shooting guns, and cruising around in an old Jeep Wagoneer where I learned to drive at the ripe old age of twelve. At the beginning it was mostly up and down Grandma's fairly long private dirt lane, or off-road through the fields and woods until I got bored with that and eventually ended on some of the local public back roads. Somehow we never got caught and I think that's a big problem with kids today—they always seem to get caught!

There were so few jobs available back then but we were young entrepreneurs and found ways to make a dollar or two by cutting grass or shoveling snow, and there was really a lot of snow back then. It would normally start in October, and you wouldn't see the ground until the following May. With a couple bucks in our pocket, we would then walk (or hitchhike) to a truck stop restaurant, order French-fries and play pinball for as long as the money held out. Eventually we got bounced out of there by some trucker bullies, so that was the end of that.

After turning sixteen I got my first real job working at the local gas station. The pay was eighty cents an hour and included mopping floors and cleaning the bathroom, tools, and best of all the garbage trucks. They had four and it was a nasty business cleaning garbage trucks for eighty cents an hour, but eventually through hard work and diligence I was promoted to working part-time on the back of one, and got a twenty-cent raise. Friends would tease me: "How's the pay, two bucks an hour and all you can eat?"

I always hated that. *Not even close to two bucks*, I would think, but nobody complained back then. It was full-time work in the summer, but after school started, I would report in the mornings from four until seven, shower and head off to school, then go back to work afterward to finish my normal chores around the garage. Oftentimes I would be working well into the evening which left absolutely no time for Joe, so I eventually started looking around for something better.

My next big break came through a friend's mother who was managing the Walden Bookstore at our local shopping mall, and she offered me a job. The only catch was I had to cut my hair, however, by this time I was already starting to flex my young teenage rebel wings. I'd had it "clean up to here" with silly useless rules we had to follow at the garage, in school, and everywhere else, so I said, *screw that*. The next day I cut my hair and took the job. It was less hours but a forty-cent raise and I could hardly imagine my good fortune.

I need to interrupt myself for a minute to explain something: As mentioned already, I was, at the time, still an adamant reader of books, finding great escape between the covers of great adventures that could free the mind by taking us to faraway places for a while.

The new bookstore job truly was a godsend; a bookworm's heaven. Shortly after that I also ran into an old friend from the garage, a fellow garbologist, and he was excited to tell me his girlfriend had just bought a big new house with a spare room for rent. It was cheap and I could move in anytime.

They were Dave and Margi, super kind people and leftovers from the late sixties hippy revolution who had finally decided to settle down and plant some roots, and very soon after that I was adopted. I had also just lost my car in an unfortunate parental divorce, which was a big problem, but not for long as they sold me their old Honda 450 motorcycle (on a payment plan) so I could continue working and finish high school.

Wonderful souls who came into my life at such critical times were a blessing that would follow me through some other difficult situations in later years. People with pure and absolute kindness that took me in and mentally nursed me back to good health without expecting any little thing in return.

Dave and Margi's was also a fun place to live and I fit right in, but all too soon it was over. Graduation was coming up and by coincidence another trashy (but famous) old movie had just come out in theaters: *Easy Rider*, a movie about some freewheeling outlaw bikers. It was so bad that we watched it at least three times and I could hardly wait to quit my job and take off on an adventure of my own. I had spent a little time on camping trips to Canada when I was younger and had made some friends there, so the plan was simple: quit my job at the bookstore and head for Ontario, and that's what I did. I was hoping for a little fun time before diving into "real life." How little I knew at that time what real life really meant, and how I was already there. Gas was around sixty cents a gallon. I had thirty-eight dollars in my pocket, so off I went. I can so dearly remember Margi holding on to Dave with tears in her eyes as we said goodbye–she was so proud!

That summer turned out to be all I had hoped for. I even met up with an old girlfriend there and almost brought her back home with me, but fortunately we both came to our senses in the nick of time. Otherwise you wouldn't be reading this right now as I'm quite sure her father would have killed me…

After the "summer of fun" was over, I began working on two separate and seasonal apprenticeships: one in a furniture restoration shop, and the other living on a farm while working a carpentry apprenticeship. Part way into this I ran into a friend who was working at a big Westinghouse factory in Pittsburgh, and he was bragging about all the money they made while basically sitting around on their rear-ends all day. This all sounded too good to be true, but I was curious and went there to put in an application. It turned out that they were not hiring at the time, but just as I was leaving I ran into an old neighbor/friend from Manor who happened to be head of the personnel department. We went back inside to his office where he explained two options: I could start immediately in maintenance, pushing a broom around, or wait until September when a new machinist apprenticeship program was starting that had better pay and more advancement opportunities. I chose the latter, however by the time September rolled around I was working back at the farm again and couldn't bring myself to quit that for a job which included driving into the city every day, even for the fantastic pay it offered. And do you know what happened after that? Within a very short few years the factory completely shut down, leaving hundreds of workers unemployed, so I had inadvertently made the right decision.

It was also around this time the next "guardian angel" came along in the form of an older Swedish lady, Ruth. She and her husband, Bill, had a little rental house that I heard about from a friend and it was perfect timing, as I happened to be sleeping in the back seat of my car. It wasn't a very big car, plus it wasn't very dependable, so I kept it parked in an abandoned lot beside the building of my winter job, which was at the furniture restoration shop.

Ruth and Bill had had a bad experience with a previous renter, another young, wayward guy like me, I suppose. They didn't need the extra money and were very sincere in wishing me good luck, but said, "Sorry, this place is no longer for rent." Instead of taking no for an answer, I went back a couple days later with a plan. I had recently been denied a car loan from my bank, which I was in desperate need of, so I began going back in to reapply every few days and bothered them so much, they finally passed me off to the president. He also politely explained why they couldn't give me the loan, but I was never one for taking no for an answer, so I returned to see him every few days to make my case. It was Mr. Parry, a sweet and kind older man who I later on became friends with, and one day either out of kindness or irritation, he finally broke down and approved the loan.

So with this lesson in mind, I continued to bother Bill and Ruth until they finally relented as well. It was a very small, but comfortable, two-room shack at eighty dollars a month, and things were starting to look up. Almost from the beginning they would invite me for dinner to which I always made excuses and politely declined, but they eventually wore me down as well.

To say I didn't have a lot of money at this time would be an understatement; I was squeaking by and wasting away on a very small salary from the furniture shop. A short time later I admitted myself to the hospital with severe stomach problems, but after a few days of testing, combined with an intravenous protein drip and some regular steady meals, I very much improved and it was determined to be a simple case of malnutrition. (It was actually way more serious than that but the problem wouldn't reoccur until a few years later when it required surgery.)

Ruth, of course, already knew that I was wasting away but never said a word, she simply continued to invite me up for meals and I never again refused. Eventually I ended up becoming a fixture in their kitchen and didn't realize until many years later that it was a soul kitchen as well. They were both good listeners, and sometimes I would go on and on about something that just happened, or I didn't understand, even angry on occasion, with a big mess in my head. They very clearly understood, however, and Ruth was always first to speak: "Here, Joe, have some more rice pudding, it's the last day and I don't want to throw it away." Then she would wait until my mouth was full and causally mention something like, "Well, Joe, maybe there is another way to look at this, what about …?"

They also had a fairly large garage-type building on the property and agreed to let me set up a little woodshop to make some extra money. "Moonlighting" is what we called it back then, and that's a pretty fair description.

Many nights I would be out there working on something until very late, and sometimes Bill would bring me out a coffee and poke around, helping me for a while. Somehow he instinctively knew which of the small picky details I didn't like to do and would zero right into them. With both of us puttering away on something, he would tell me stories about when he was young and just starting out—some of them very interesting—and we both enjoyed passing the time while picking away on some antique piece of furniture.

One day I began to wonder how I could ever repay them for everything – feeding me, cheap rent, and now free labor in my new woodworking enterprise, so finally I just asked him. Bill got a little smile on his face and I suddenly realized he had been waiting (or hoping) for this very question. He explained how sometimes in life somebody will reach out to help you and there will be no possible way to ever repay them, so the only way is for you to help somebody else later on when you're in a position to do so. Without knowing it, I was on the path to understanding mentorship and it's something I carry with me to this very day.

There is another very personal part that I should mention here, Bill and Ruth had lost a young son a few years earlier, and somehow my being there helped them calm the terrible memory, Bill especially. For me, I was carrying around a lot of anger and confusion at the time about some things that happened previously, (nothing like the tragedy they had experienced of course), but much of this misguided emotion was rapidly melting away.

My short time there in Middletown happened so long ago but made such an impact on my young life that I still find comfort in the memory, and sometimes even solutions to difficult or confusing situations come from my experiences during that time. I still remember them both in my prayers and from time to time will go somewhere quiet and talk to Ruth. When life gets crazy, difficult, or even sad I always find great comfort in remembering her words: "Well, Joe, maybe there's another way to look at this."

Over the next several years I worked in the carpentry trade and eventually formed my own little construction company. Most of the business was residential building and improvements, with some light commercial mixed in, but the thing I enjoyed most was building houses. It was a rewarding occupation; in the beginning there was nothing, and a short time later a new structure would appear and change the landscape forever. I especially enjoyed working with blueprints and building schematics, and looking back I realize how helpful this was in developing a three-dimensional perspective that would come to serve me well in later years. Throughout this time I also still managed to maintain a small furniture shop in the evenings, but it was difficult as most of the time we were buried in construction projects pretty much year-round.

I haven't been back to our little Manor very many times since childhood, but recently a small carving job came up for a lady just outside of town. I recognized the name, but couldn't quite make the connection until she invited me in for lunch and the mystery was solved.

A sit down and prepared meal is always a most appreciated gesture, and I especially enjoyed having a chance to chat to someone about their life and family. Plus it always surprised me how some people are willing to open up and share very personal stories with a complete stranger. However, I soon discovered that we were not at all complete strangers when she laid out a peanut butter sandwich with potato chips and chocolate milk (my favorite childhood comfort food) and said, "You don't remember me do you, Joey King?"

I cringed a bit and sunk a little deeper in my chair in anticipation of what would come next. Only two kinds of people call me Joey: kids I grew up with, and close family members. She was neither, but had been a substitute teacher and overall volunteer in our elementary school, and one particular day they had a field trip planned to visit the Pittsburgh Zoo. She hadn't been scheduled to come along, but was asked at the last minute to fill in for somebody else who couldn't make it. The only problem was it was going to be a really long day and everyone had to bring a lunch bag as there were no other options at this point in time. She went on to explain how we ended up sitting together on the bus and I shared my lunch with her, and how much it was appreciated as she had no chance to prepare anything ahead of time, and also missed breakfast that morning, and I saved the day!

She was correct about me not remembering any of this but after that day I very clearly remembered her daughter, Lois. She was probably the smartest kid in our class, and we shared a common bond because everybody made fun of our names.

For her it was 'Lois Lane', Superman's girlfriend of course, and me; Joe King, or simply 'Joking' as in, "Oh, you must be joking?" Since we're already on the subject of names and it seems relevant at this point, I need to interrupt myself and go a bit deeper.

My Christian name is Joseph Thomas King, named after my two grandfathers: Joseph Lukasiewicz, and Thomas King. It had been decided ahead of time that I would be Thomas Joseph, but then I was coincidentally born on Grandpa Joseph's birthday, so they switched it at the last minute. I hardly ever tell that story because somebody always comes back with you know what; "oh surely you're joking."

Well back to the carving story: It turned out to be a really nice day and so enjoyable to hear some stories from way back then, plus I was touched that she remembered that story after all those years and took the time to share it with me. Afterward I drove into town and parked near where the old train station used to sit, just across the road from Elsie's Diner and Davorsky's Costume Shop. This was the school's main bus stop where we congregated twice a day and for many of us a twenty-minute walk each way. This was also the place where we could hop on a train to visit girls in the next town and I remember my father growling at me one time: "Why do you go chasing girls all over the country when you have the prettiest little thing right next door?" It's true, she was pretty, but the next town wasn't actually all over the country, and you know how things like that go when you're young and full of adventure.

And wouldn't he be surprised that I would end up with a girl from halfway around the world? But this shouldn't have been any surprise to anybody. My parents had a big station wagon car with a tow-along camping trailer, and every weekend of the summer was spent in some remote state forest campground. We would also take off for three to four weeks at a time traveling to some new part of the country, so by the age of fifteen I had been to all four corners: from Florida to California, Texas to Canada, and so many places in-between. Looking back on all this, it's really quite plain to see that I came by the travel bug legitimately. Plus I've also managed to pass it on to my own kids and proud to see them passing it along as well.

Bailey, Pap and Jasmine

The Tongass Narrows, Ketchikan, Alaska, 2005.
Twenty minutes after this photo was taken all work would
grind to a halt as the tide continued rising and I was forced
to retreat. We would attach sturdy I-bolts somewhere on
the poles and rope them off, otherwise by the next
morning they're well on their way to Japan. Notice the
fairly calm water? This wasn't normal and on certain days
the wind could blow my little saw off and into the water,
or even knock me off balance so I had to be ever mindful
of little details like that.

Three

Ketchikan ...

It was another hot, muggy mid-August afternoon in the mountains and another sudden cloudburst emerged, lasting just long enough to completely saturate everything, including our spirits. Ten minutes later it cleared up and everything was all lovely again, but not really. With temperatures hovering in the mid to upper nineties, the cool rain was refreshing, however, by the time we got all the wood and tools uncovered, it was like a sauna, plus the deer flies and mosquitoes returned in droves.

We were well into a house building project, my new house actually, and those sudden soakers were frustrating as hell, and happening at least three or four times a day. One time my buddy Mike winked at me and said, "Well, Joe, keeps the dust down, eh?"

On one of our unscheduled breaks, the phone rang; it was a lady calling to ask if I would be interested in coming over to carve some totem poles at their place in Ketchikan, to which I politely responded, "Ketch-a-what?" Over the years I got a fair number of inquiries from the West Coast, but most of the time it didn't pan out. Still, it was good business to treat each and every one seriously, which of course I did. Right up front I mentioned that there were a number of carvers in the upper Northwest Pacific region, but she already knew that and replied, "We live on an island, so it's a plane ride for everybody."

Her next question was if I had any experience carving totem poles, to which I replied; "Some, but very limited, and to be honest I really don't understand them and so far I have yet to make one I'm happy with."

Somehow I had inadvertently said the right thing; they were looking for someone who could copy things well and work from drawings and models of their own designs. The next thing I knew I was on a plane to Ketchikan, Alaska, which began one of the greatest carving adventures of my life.

Sometimes I speak in analogies and here's one: You could see a hundred pictures of the Grand Canyon, but never even begin to realize or appreciate how absolutely huge and spectacular it is until you see in person for the first time and it takes your breath away. Southeast Alaska and totem poles are kind of like that too; you could never truly begin to understand or appreciate what they are until you visit the place where they originated in context to the Pacific Northwest. Similar to many other examples throughout the history of indigenous people who came from a certain area or region that was so rich in natural environmental resources that they didn't need to spend every waking minute of the day just sustaining themselves. In other words; they had some free time to make art. This is something I had read much about and studied prior to then, but didn't fully grasp the concept until stepping off a boat and landing right smack in the middle of totem ground zero.

The physical journey was also interesting and included three different airplanes, two separate boats (not counting a short channel ferry) a couple car rides on either end, around twenty-four hours door to door.

The people I was working for dropped me off at a cabin on a little island in the middle of several bigger islands, and right across a small bay from another little island where I would be doing the work. I have such a clear memory of that moment, sitting there on my duffel bag as their skiff drifted away and staring out into the inky black night, just taking in all the new and unfamiliar sounds and smells to be found near the ocean. Eventually I stirred back to life and found a stone path leading up to the cabin which would be my new home for the next couple of weeks. After getting a fire going in the woodstove, I poured a nightcap and went back outside to wonder in amazement at the most incredible night sky I had ever seen.

Southeast Alaska is classified as a coastal rain forest and can easily exceed two hundred inches of rain per year, plus it geographically sits on a latitude that boasts the third-highest tides in North America. This amounts to twenty feet or more during certain seasons, so the people who lived there needed to pay close attention to tide charts (which are always included in the weather reports), and for good reason. For example, part of the bay I crossed every morning would either flood, or completely empty out and become a rocky mudflat as the water moved in and out at regular intervals, and this happened twice a day. Each ebb and flow lasted for a very short time and I had to be ever mindful of securing the boat, otherwise by morning it could be well on its way to Japan. All the docks there used a sliding "post and ring" system, which allowed for the extreme rising and falling water levels, but I had no such convenience at the cabin and always had to improvise.

I need to sidetrack for a moment to expand on this type of demographical phenomenon a bit more. The Bay of Fundy is located on the northeast coast of America and straddles the US and Canadian border, and also boasts the highest tides in North America. (Anchorage, Alaska, is a close second.)

In extreme conditions, this can be up to twenty-eight feet per day (forty feet being the record,) but the normal rise and fall is a little over half of that, which is still pretty substantial. Keep in mind that every vertical foot up or down equates to huge volumes of water moving horizontally as well, in, then back out again, which can fill or empty bays and inlets of any size twice a day. For example, the first time I saw the Bay of Fundy, it was beautiful, stretching out for a great distance and framing the city off in the distance, then a few hours later it was transformed into a massive and somewhat unsightly mudflat. You didn't have to go far in any direction from there to find other examples of the effects of such enormous amounts of water colliding with itself while changing directions twice a day. Huge whirlpools the size of football fields would develop just offshore and could and would easily swallow small boats. Some of the first fish farms were actually started there, taking advantage of the steady flushing motion. They work by put big netting-enclosed underwater corrals where the fish are raised and kept until they're ready for harvest. Today you'll find a choice between wild-caught or farm-raised salmon in most grocery stores. Wild-caught is mostly from the Pacific, while farm-raised is largely an Atlantic product.

And here's the difference: Fat-flightless farm-raised chickens are by far tastier than their wild counterparts, but salmon, however, are exactly the opposite. Wild-caught is far superior to farm-raised, and knowing that we should all sleep better tonight!

Waking up each day in my cozy little one-room cabin I was greeted by such an incredible panoramic view like few other places I had seen in the world. The skyline was ever changing, regardless of the time of day. Oftentimes it would rain heavily throughout the night, making way for a thick blanket of early morning fog, and have you ever heard the expression "so thick you could cut it with a knife?" That is a pretty accurate description. But sometimes when the clear blue sky would break through, it was like an explosion of color reflecting off the water, and I discovered another anomaly I had also previously read about. In certain directions you could take a photo, then turn it upside down and nobody would notice the difference. Rotate the same photo ninety degrees and it can sometimes resemble a totem pole. Evening skies were especially wonderful, first turning a dark, bruised purple with bursts of bright sunshine streaking through while continuously changing direction and angles from minute to minute. Absolute magic. The forest across the bay would seemingly undulate in shades of deep green to brown while the cloud cover slowly melted from purple into black, and very soon after that everything would disappear altogether.

The back side of the cabin was quite different, however, you couldn't see more than fifty feet in any direction as it quickly transformed into a lush multilayered rain forest with moss covering everything close to the ground.

There were trees literally growing on top of each other. The only place it was possible to walk around and explore was along the shore at low tide, or a couple very small trails going off into the thicket, which I soon discovered were nothing more than bear trails leading to and from the annual salmon buffet. And it was not easy walking; they were very low to the ground with many obstacles, so you had to stoop over most of the time, all the while mindful that you were walking on a bear trail.

Eventually I got braver and began exploring more of them, each time taking the dog along for an early warning device, and a rifle pointed straight ahead just in case. The owners were livid when they found out about this, and I quote: "Ted doesn't like it because we can always find another carver, but it takes months to train a new dog."

It didn't take long to find a good working routine, waking up very early to get sorted for the day with coffee first, followed by twenty minutes of exercise. Then I would fry up a hearty breakfast, eat, and make my way across the bay to work on the poles. The cabin was completely solar-powered, which was primarily used for lighting, a radio with only one AM channel, and a small black-and-white television that could only play cassette videos.

I had two boats to choose from: a small, motorized fishing boat, and an even smaller old wooden rowboat, which was my preference on calm mornings, and when the weather allowed. In the wee hours of morning all of the surrounding wildlife was waking up as well, and the first sounds were that of bald eagle families who were nesting all around the bay.

Sometimes they made funny gurgling sounds as though communicating amongst themselves. There was also a pair nesting in the old Sitka spruce tree growing right up against my cabin, and each day I would see them looking down at me as I came and went. Halfway through rowing across the bay I would stop, drift along, and listen to all the sounds echoing back and forth like a soft, natural symphony. No doubt they were communicating among themselves and I often wondered if maybe I was the topic of conversation. "Yep, he's not from around here; I give him a week."

Eagle nest above my cabin.

As in many other coastal regions around the world, most everything there revolves around the sea, and I would be working with giant Western red cedar trees that were floated in, then strategically put in place according to the local tide chart. Over sixty percent of land in Alaska is owned by the federal government, but if a big tree falls into the ocean, for example, it's fair game for anybody skilled or crazy enough to cut and harvest it.

By the time they came to me, most of them would be quite waterlogged, extremely dense, and way too heavy to move, even with a big tractor. So all we could do at that point was to use big heavy railroad car jacks to rotate or adjust them slightly for carving. The guy who brought those logs didn't have a very big boat, but something he did have was one of the biggest dogs I've ever seen. Cujo was a cross between a Saint Bernard and some type of Siberian breed, and he was always perched right on the bow, which made him look that much bigger. Mike, the boat owner, was a man of few words, like most Alaskans I suppose, and one day I tried to make a joke: "So Mike, how much would you charge to bring one of these logs to Pittsburgh for me?" Scratching his chin and thinking for a moment he replied: "Thirty-five dollars an hour."

They were wonderful logs from a carver's view: Big, long, straight Western red cedar, which, along with hemlock, pretty much dominated the area. I would be working with the owner's designs, a seemingly simple process but a huge learning curve nevertheless. As I soon came to discover, every little innuendo had some type of meaning, and much of that was open to interpretation. Plus all the while big tides were constantly moving in and out in and around my carving area, so I had to pay constant close attention to those as well. Sometimes it was fairly calm, but more often there was a driving coastal wind dumping up to five inches of rain per day, which also took a bit of getting used to.

Working on large sculptures normally included a combination of intricate details mixed in with long boring cuts, so during the calm spells I would work on the small, easier sections. Then when it really howled I would hunker down into a firm three-point stance with my back to the wind and do the heavy grunt work. The only times I had to actually stop working was when storms would bring in an unexpected "bastard tide," where the water would rise too fast and flood the area. To cut a long story short, I was both mentally and physically firing on all cylinders and loving every minute of it.

While working on the various designs, one day I recalled an incident from several years prior that occurred while doing a commission for a large university installation project (CMU, Pittsburgh). My part was carving three abstract feminine-type totem poles. The sketch they provided me with was a bit unclear and somehow I got one of them mixed up, confusing the front with the back. After a slightly embarrassing moment and a few minor adjustments, I was able to turn it around and eventually it did turn out okay. I tended to be more cautious about things like that at this time, but there were some similar incidents while working on the Alaskan poles, only it was an upside-down issue as opposed to front to back, a common mistake among pole carvers, as I came to understand.

It's Kitten, by my side every minute of the day. I let her sleep in my cabin one night and found out later that it was the first and only time in her life she ever slept indoors. (my bad!) Another time my dog was a huge Newfoundlander, or 'Newfie' and they are of a herder breed, so anytime you're walking beside them they instinctively try pushing you to one side or another. This is a fun and interesting fact I didn't know about, fun except when you're walking out to the boat and halfway down the dock they start nudging you off to the side. All fun and games until somebody goes in the water...

Many of the Indigenous art designs originated from images reflecting on the water, relating to the way Indigenous people navigated their lives in and around such a hostile environment. For example; they rarely ventured far into the forest, no real need for that because everything necessary for survival was right there in front of them. But when working on new pole designs, there were so many other little innuendos that could be critical as well. Things like, "Was she wearing a hat?" could turn into a long and sometimes contentious discussion, which normally ended up in a simple yes or no nod of the head.

I should take a moment to describe the people I was working for. Close your eyes and try to imagine a true Alaskan frontiersman and it's him. Handsome but rugged, and truly one of the most clever and hardest working men I've ever met. One time he cut his hand pretty bad and I knew it was going to require stitches, plus I also knew he wasn't going to make the long boat trip to a hospital, so I offered to do it for him. He simply shook his head and said, "No, no, I'll do it myself." Their home, designed and built himself, was located on a small private island along with a personal workshop. This included both a metal machining and woodworking area, which were both fully set up with the most modern and efficient equipment available, and all run on solar power (with a backup generator, of course). He was also a prolific inventor of things both big and small and very much reminded me of Captain Nemo from the classic movie. On occasion he shared some personal stories like the time he built a floatplane for his kids so they could go around fishing in the nearby small mountain lakes.

Other little details he would mention in passing, like one of his sons was the youngest person ever to fly solo in an Alaskan floatplane at the age of thirteen, which for many years probably meant youngest in the world.

They have a local term in Alaska, *Totemology*, the study of totem poles, but it hasn't quite made its way into the dictionary yet. This related mostly to general or specific designs and customs surrounding the carving and placement according to local customs. It also covers the strict rules regarding the actual carvers themselves, for example, any new pole had to be crafted entirely by Indigenous people in order to be completely legitimate. In modern times it can be a bit more flexible as many different people will lay hands on a finished pole from beginning to completion.

First the giant logs needed to be cut and moved to a good carving location, then moved again at least one more time before placement in its permanent location. That part could sometimes include non-indigenous helpers such as a native-born Alaskans, and was occasionally overlooked, but some white guy with a chainsaw from Pittsburgh that arrived on an airplane? Plus keep in mind it was not a very big island with a year-round population of around eight thousand, and one local radio station. It was a bit strange my first time there when it felt at times like they were hiding me out, and that's exactly what they were doing. They were building a very cool park that was very much connected to the tourist industry, and boasted upward of a million tourists passing through each summer. The last thing they wanted was for it to end up on the local radio talk show, so they made me promise not to share anything on the Internet. It actually made perfect sense once I understood and I have changed their names in this book out of respect for that.

Keep in mind there was no cell phone service on the island, and even a landline was complicated and had to be bounced off a friend's house closer to the main island, but was still notably unreliable. Cable television was also non-existent, so the little radio station was truly my only link to the outside world. I actually started looking forward to the regular news and variety shows with their localized and somewhat novice reporting. The weather always came first, with small craft advisories, then reports on the occasional missing floatplane or fishing boat, and ferry cancellations, which were of the greatest importance.

Most of the islands had their own school but were very small, and extra curriculum activities like band or sports teams commonly had to ferry across to neighboring islands in order to have enough players for a whole team. Can you imagine, as a parent, listening to the forecast and wondering if the storm was bad enough to cancel football practice that night? And of course there were politics to report on as well. Ted Stevens, the state senator, was in some kind of trouble at the time, plus the governor, Sarah Palin, was also under attack for her participation in the "Bridge to Nowhere" controversy. Any and all public figures were, of course, beaten to death on daily talk shows, as was expected. Each morning during the tourist season they would list all the different cruise ships coming in overnight and docking for the day so local business owners knew what size of staff to schedule. I traveled there five times over a span of nine years to work on the poles and that little inside slice of local island life was one of my overall best memories.

My favorite part of the entire experience, however, was going off to explore after the working day was finished. You didn't need to go far in any direction to find strange, new, unusual and interesting things to look at. There was an incredible amount of amazing animals and marine life, and all right there in close proximity. Those big crazy tides that I mentioned before were the result of strong ocean currents funneling into and between the islands, producing such a unique and hearty ecosystem like nowhere else on the planet. A simple comparison is when wind is compressed and accelerated between buildings in a coastal city center, and the velocity is greatly increased.

It's the same with water, and in southeast Alaska

it's the warm Japanese ocean current pushing everything around, which in turn makes it a rain forest, as opposed to a snowy tundra. (Similar to the UK, which is also far north enough for heavy snow, but the warm Atlantic Ocean currents turn most of the precipitation to rain.) The end result is an incredibly oxygen-enriched environment where both land and aquatic life thrive. Plus the channels between islands are extremely deep in many places, so it was not uncommon to see a pod of orcas passing through and following the tides. During low tide was an entirely different situation as the receding water melted away exposing a variety of rock-clinging crustaceans like most of us only see in photos and nautical museums. One time something very odd and curious happened just offshore; it looked like big pieces of rope slapping around in the air, and as it turns out, it was nothing more than a pack of sea otters attacking a giant octopus. Salmon season is an especially busy time; it's an absolute feeding frenzy which brings out every bear in the forest, and humans from the lower forty eight as well.

Fishing, both commercial and recreational, thrived there and remain a huge part of the local economy today. It was mostly salmon and halibut, and people came from everywhere imaginable, hiring outfitters to take them out in droves during the regular season. They also had most everything down to a science. For example, at the end of the trip they filleted and shrink-wrapped the catch, flash froze them, and packed them in dry ice boxes for the trip home, and I swear sometimes there were more fish on the plane than people.

And this is no exaggeration, a big part of Alaska Airline's 737 fleet was actually fitted out for cargo and was easy to spot as there were no windows in the front half of the fuselage. All the people sat toward the back, while business class on that type of plane were headed for somebody's grill.

Back to the poles. Eventually I discovered there were actually ways to officially sanctify a finished and installed totem pole, which, in our case, was in the form of a "potlatch." If this word reminds you of the old American traditional potluck party where everybody brings a dish, it's because it's exactly the same thing and most likely where our term originated. Ketchikan is demographically located near the middle of the inner Northwest Passage, which the locals simply refer to as the *Tongass Narrows*. This is also home to a number of various indigenous tribes from the region; towns and villages include the Haida, Tlingit, and Tsimshian, and a few other smaller groups. All were invited to the potlatch, and often the events had almost a thousand attendees. This, of course, included all the elders representing each different village, and at some point during the day they all weighed in. If it was a nice pole, well made with an interesting story (and they were enjoying the potlatch), and all were in approval, the highest-ranking elder would rub his right hand in a pan of red paint (actually more like ochre), then make an imprint on the base, and it was now sanctioned as traditional.

I am skimming over a lot of interesting details here, but suffice to say how fortunate it was to have come across such a rare experience like this, to catch a small glimpse of such an amazing wonderful indigenous art form, and observe where it first originated in both a geographical and historical context.

My 'Newfie' watching over the progress and patiently waiting for our coffee break, and his half of the sandwich.

Four

Pine Hollow…

It was a Friday, I think, and I was sitting in an attorney's office with Stuart Kline to complete a property deed transfer, and I was very excited about it. Just a few short months before I had rented a very old gas station from him that included the first two months free to clean the place up. Stuart definitely got the better part of the deal as it was a complete mess and very much in disrepair, but with a little love and a lot of work I had known it would make a great studio.

Just about the time we got the old place back on its feet, Stu stopped in one day to tell me the bad news: he was declaring personal bankruptcy and needed to sell the property as soon as possible. He said not to worry, because he wanted me to have it and we would work it all out. This included a down payment, then monthly mortgage payments made directly to him until the full sale price was met, and there we were, in the office signing all the papers. At some point the attorney, who looked to be around the same age as Stuart, looked up and said, "Oh, it's December 7th. Where were you?" Stu said he was already enlisted and stationed in California. The attorney nodded his head and said that he had enlisted a month later, and it took a moment before I realized it was the anniversary of Pearl Harbor and they were remembering a time back in 1941 when America was ushered into World War II. It was so interesting to watch how their demeanor suddenly changed as they exchanged a few brief memories with each other and realized it was exactly fifty years later, to the day.

Top photo is of the original owner, whom I purchased the
property from for ten thousand dollars in 1991. The
bottom photo was taken just prior to restoring the
building.

So there it was. Finally my longtime dream of a public studio came true in the shape of a seventy-five-year-old run-down Exxon gas station. Brought back from the edge of extinction, it was going to change my life in ways I could never have imagined. This place, as I soon discovered, had many different lives along the way and had evolved from a petrol pumping station and local convenience store before eventually becoming a rental home. By the time I came along it was had been known for over ten years as "Uncle Bob's."

Uncle Bob wasn't actually the only tenant, just the last and longest person to live there. I was told this by a year a complete stranger who would stop by once a year, look around, make some small talk, and say, "I used to live here a long time ago." Keep in mind the place had no running water, just an old-fashioned well pump, and a nasty old outhouse around back. As time went by I began to get to know Uncle Bob through all the stories and unusual objects he had left behind.

The small main structure had four separate lean-to-type additions, all filled with junk accumulated over a long time, which we burned for weeks in epic bonfires that would smolder for days afterward. One time I noticed a lot of homemade bird feeders around the property, then later started finding little peepholes on the inside of the building strategically located at points directly across from each individual feeder. Plus there were old homemade whiskey, wine, and moonshine bottles laying around everywhere, which started to paint a picture.

Old Uncle Bob—one-legged Uncle Bob, I should add—didn't go very far, and his favorite pastime was obviously getting tanked and watching birds.

Everything old and nasty was eventually cleared away and it started to feel like a carving studio more and more each day. *My* carving studio. The only surviving remnant was the old outhouse. Nobody wanted to go near it and we didn't know what to do, so one day I simply put a match to it, which probably wasn't the best idea as there were overhead power lines running pretty close to it. At first it seemed to be going OK, so I put my headphones on and went back to working on a special order I had just received, when all of a sudden I got this creepy feeling, like somebody was watching me. I slowly turned around and it was like a scene out of a disaster movie. The property was completely surrounded with fire trucks and police cruisers, and standing directly behind me were two anxious-looking policeman waiting for me to shut the saw off.

I thought, *Uh-oh*, but it turned out OK, they were only a little bit mad, and after they put the fire out all the firemen came inside to look at the carvings. I actually sold one (and an old chainsaw I was also looking to get rid of), plus received an order for another. I also made friends with some of the policemen who were equally curious about what was happening to Uncle Bob's old place. From then on some of them would stop by from time to time to see what was new.

Pine Hollow Road forked off to the right of the main busy road in the front, so my place sat on a triangle-shaped property with a small office supply business on one side, and a little farm directly across the big road.

There was also a residential neighborhood just around the bend and I eventually became friends with many of the surrounding people in the little community. There was never a dull moment, and over time the place also gathered quite a bit of public attention as well. Quite often I was featured in local newspapers and had a number of television spots. (Close to a hundred times, I would estimate.)

The little farm directly across the main from me belonged to a fellow named Quinn. He had quite a few smaller domesticated animals and occasionally some of them would wander over, including live peacocks. Some of them, however, didn't quite make it across the busy road. Chickens were the hardest hit (no pun intended) but did eventually work it out and stopped crossing altogether. The pigs, however, were fast learners and had better luck, however, one day three of them stopped right in the middle of the busy intersection and traffic began backing up in all directions. I thought the best way to remedy the situation was to try and scare them back over with a chainsaw running full on, so I started to wave it around at them, which actually didn't work. Once again I got that creepy feeling like someone was watching, and glancing over my shoulder it was Nancy. She was sitting in her truck and slowly shaking her head like *is this really happening?* There also happened to be a newspaper reporter stuck in the traffic jam, which of course I hadn't noticed, so the very next day, on the second page, was a photo and little story about some crazy guy chasing the three little pigs with a chainsaw in front of Uncle Bob's old place.

Late one night I was working on some last minute Christmas orders and just closing up when I heard someone at the door. It was not quite a knock, but more like a creepy scratching noise. Flinging the door open I instantly found myself face-to-face with a huge, elderly Billy goat. It had a long scraggly beard, giant curved horns, and really bad breath. (Yes, it was that close.) He didn't seem at all friendly and caught me off guard, so I instantly stepped back a couple of paces and he took advantage and barged right in. I was now on the defense and not sure what he was going to do next, as he slowly backed me into a corner. Keep in mind this all happened in mere seconds and the situation was rapidly becoming critical and downright scary. In a moment of self-survival brilliance, I was able to grab a big, heavy furniture clamp from the work bench and wacked him right on the head as hard as I could. Surprisingly, this hardly fazed him, but a moment of confusion allowed me gain control of the situation just long enough to grab him by the horns, push him back out the door, and save myself.

After taking a few minutes to regain my composure, I found Quinn's work number and let him know that the friggin goat was at my studio, and asked if he would mind coming over to get it. "Sure no problem," he said, "but whatever you do, don't let him in; he's kinda mean."

The absolute, most helpful support all through my time there came from my longtime best friend, Mike Jones. He helped enormously with the initial set up of the property, then stayed on for one or two days a week for pretty much the duration of my time there.

After a while we worked together like an old married couple, anticipating the response to a question before it was even asked. Some of his duties would include chip removal and pile management, painting the carvings, tidying up the place, greeting customers, and answering the phone. One day I overheard him taking a call but only caught bits and pieces, which went something like this: "Yes, yes, no thank you, no we don't have a phone, yes and you too, goodbye." He explained that it was a telemarketer for a long-distance phone company and we were both a bit surprised that she believed him about not having a phone. That was Mike, always the gentleman and never had a negative word for anyone, (not even a parasitic telemarketer) and he's been that way for as long as I've known him.

As mentioned earlier, the property didn't have running water and since I had already burned the old outhouse, it started to become somewhat of a problem to perform, how should I say this, certain daily functions. Mike took it upon himself to resolve the problem. Keeping in mind this was a triangle-shaped property with busy roads on two of the three sides, he found a good spot toward the back and started piling and standing up logs to form a seven-foot-high, very rustic, walled-in little fortress-looking room.

The year was 2000, so he affectionately named it "the new millennial shithouse." We had long since become friends with the folks across the other road and had full access to their modern indoor facilities, but the new millennium shithouse was certainly a most convenient (and appreciated) improvement for day-to-day studio life.

Another clever improvisation we had was the phone alert system. They make a small device for deaf people who cannot hear a phone ring, kind of like us when the chain saws were blasting away. It's quite simple, actually, we just plugged this small unit into a normal electrical outlet, then plugged a lamp directly into that and it would blink on and off in conjunction with the phone ringing. We took this one step farther and strung Christmas lights all around in place of a lamp, and from then on it was always great fun to get a phone call and see all the party lights blinking away.

One time, however, I nearly burned the place down. There was a little tool called a burnzomatic torch, which was mainly used by plumbers for soldering purposes, but I used it for darkening and highlighting finished carving features. One day I was just finishing up with that and started removing the tip from the gas tank for safety reasons, and didn't notice there was still a tiny flame in the very tip. So halfway unscrewed, the whole thing ignited in my hands like a little burning inferno. I instantly dropped it onto the floor and tried to kick it out the door, but it missed the door and bounced back into a pile of chainsaws. The saws are normally somewhat covered in oil and gas residue from normal use, and this, in turn, instantly ignited into what was now becoming a substantial ball of fire. Within a few heartbeats it was out of control and rapidly turning into a big burning inferno and threatening to burn down the studio. My mind raced to remember where the fire extinguisher was and suddenly I realized it was in the back room, so now a split-second decision presented itself: Take a chance of finding it in time, or run for my life.

I knew it was somewhere in the back room, but I would be completely trapped if I couldn't find it in time. Fortunately I *was* able to find it and managed to put the fire out in time, then went outside and tried to calm down before my chest exploded…

Sometimes an old friend from the past would find me and drop in for a visit. Joe Nimitz, for example, was a regular and a more interesting and colorful person- would be hard to find. I was pretty young when we first met. He had a business in an old but completely restored barn-like museum called Suzie's Antique Barn. I was just starting out at the time with a little furniture restoration shop not far from there, so naturally I gravitated to this most interesting place. From a historical perspective, this was a period in time just before the antique business in America exploded. Joe had a demolition business in Pittsburgh and was tearing down old city homes, some of which were still full of magnificent old furniture, collectables, and a host of other valuable items. This also coincided with an era where many younger second-and third-generation families started moving to the suburbs into modern homes and had no use for all this old stuff. They would take a few sentimental items, then simply walk away.

But to the trained eye there were hidden treasures among all the clutter, which he turned into a little gold mine, and did quite well with it. Sometimes I would hear stories, local gossip actually, that he was a mafia hit man or international contraband dealer, and other unsavory things like that. He did very much fit the script in terms of appearance.

I had an old bench seat in the studio; it was an extra from my work van and the only piece of furniture almost big enough to stretch out on for a little nap, which he did quite often. Personally, I'm not a napping kind of guy, but Joe was and it was fun to watch him drift off to sleep in the middle of a story, then awaken a short time later and finish the story. Sometimes he told very personal stories in great detail. One example was for many years he worked for the Proctor & Gamble company representing their cleaning products, and was actually the original Mr. Clean that you might remember seeing on their bottles.

Joe was a Hungarian immigrant and came to America toward the end of the industrial revolution of which Pittsburgh was a big center. Right away he got accepted on a sports scholarship to Pitt University.

"They didn't have two teams like they do now, offense and defense, we went both ways start to finish," he would recount, half bragging and half complaining. After practice each night he would go for a swim in the nearby Monongahela River, which, I might add, was at this point in time one of the most polluted rivers in America. It was lined with steel producing factories belching coal smoke into the air, and countless tug boats pushing long lines of coke and slag-filled barges up and down the river. An industrial cesspool would sum it up mildly, but he didn't mind and on his daily swims he began to notice certain things as the landscape became more familiar. At one of the factory sites, guys were dumping wheelbarrow loads of sand over the hill, and he became curious.

As it turns out it, this was sand from brass and bronze casting molds, and upon closer inspection he started finding large chunks of these semi-valuable metals mixed in like an undiscovered mine. This was his first business in America, hauling two five-gallon buckets a very long way to a scrapyard farther up the river.

This intuition for discovering hidden treasures followed him throughout his entire life and he eventually became quite proficient. I know of one instance where he found an old flintlock gun collection from the Civil War era in an abandoned house they were demolishing. It turned out to be quite valuable and eventually sold for well over a million dollars after changing hands a couple times. He found it a house they were getting paid to tear down.

The nearby town of Irwin was my support hub during those days and had pretty much everything we needed: three restaurants, two hardware stores, a print shop, and most importantly a computer shop, which pretty much enabled many of the stories in this journal. There were a few other necessary business's including two banks: Irwin Bank and Trust, and the Union National. It was known, or believed, that the presidents of both banks were not on friendly terms as they were in direct competition, but I learned otherwise when I happened to have both in the studio at the same time.

I already knew Mr. Parry prior to this; he had given me my very first auto loan, which I mentioned earlier. The other was Mr. Kretickek, who I would come to know later on a much more personal basis. Ted, was a weekend warrior with a wood shop in his basement and had great interest in my carvings.

He actually stopped in fairly often, never for very long, but he was a funny guy and I always enjoyed his visits. The time that I happened to have both together we ended up talking about bad financial mistakes we'd all made earlier in life, and what an interesting experience it was sitting on logs with a couple bank presidents!

I went first with an incident where I had bought some property at a county tax sale on recommendation of a "friend." This turned out to be something completely different than I had anticipated and was an absolute failure. Mr. Parry snorted politely and told us he knew all about that; "Your attorney was our bank solicitor as well, and you're still wondering why I didn't want to give you that loan?"

Ted had kind of a similar story, only opposite and not such small potatoes. He lost a sizeable piece of property through a tax sale after somehow overlooking his payments. "Lost the whole damn place," he said. He glanced at his watch and suddenly got all serious. He left me with the parting words, "Listen, young man, life is short and we only get one turn in the barrel, and when it's over, it's over. So don't you ever waste one minute of your life worrying about mistakes you've made in the past; look back, but don't stare." With that he got in his car and left, and while driving off with an arm out the window, we could hear him yelling, "One turn in the barrel, son." That was some really good advice.

Behind the studio was a huge and ever-growing mountain of wood chips that piled up year after year. There were cutoffs from thousands of carvings before my time there ended.

Free wood chips were always in demand, as I soon discovered, mostly as coverage for wet ball fields, garden mulch, and some other things, so people were always coming by to fill anything from a few buckets to entire truck loads. My favorite were the old-timers (or seasoned gardeners might be a more polite description). They were the most interesting of the bunch. Those fellows always asked permission first, then found a spot around the back and bottom of the pile and dug around for some "good stuff" that was properly aged.

Whenever possible, I would clock out and sit down and chat with anybody who knew Uncle Bob, or had stories about him. He had obviously been kind of a hermit, had only one leg, as mentioned already, and really loved "his" birds. Through one of the stories I discovered that he was also Quinn's uncle, which helped explain why the farm animals were always coming over. Even after he was long gone, the place remained abundant in birdlife, which was a constant source of amusement, and sometimes I wondered if I was slowly turning into Uncle Bob...

Wild parakeets were in great abundance and one of my favorites, but they gradually dwindled in numbers after a red tail hawk family moved in nearby. Apparently they were one of Mr. Hawk's favorites too. Each summer the hawks would have a fresh brood of little ones that would practice learning to fly directly overhead, sometimes very low and I began to recognize them even after they had fully grown and moved a short distance up the Pine Hollow valley to start a new family of their own.

Sometimes during a lunch break I would take off for a quick one-mile power walk up a little nearby lane, and one day I came across the biggest great horned owl I had ever seen. I startled him off at first, but he didn't go far, so I moved quietly closer and suddenly two big hawks, *my hawks* actually, came blasting out of nowhere and started to dive bomb the giant owl. Even though Mr. Owl was much bigger, the attack was so aggressive that I feared a bad ending for all three of them. Luckily the treetop brawl didn't continue for very long as Mr. Owl soon got the message and moved on, but it was such an incredible Nature Channel moment and I'm sure Uncle Bob would have enjoyed it too.

There was always a steady stream of visitors stopping by the studio; some coming from far away and sometimes unusual places. Mike began calling it "World Headquarters." It was also right around this time when I mothballed the old typewriter and bought my first computer, which of course changed everything. They were pretty basic at that time, but it wasn't very long before the Internet became well established, and the term "World Headquarters" started to take on a new meaning. This was around 1991, and our local computer guys suggested that I start a new website for my business. Treecarver.com was born soon after. My main use for it in the beginning was simply to have an online brochure, which allowed me to move away from expensive color printing. Plus, I was already writing articles for *Chip Chats* by then, and computers also came with another really great invention: spell check.

One morning I woke up to find an email from someone wanting to order a carving, and that changed everything. Sipping on a mug of coffee while still in my pajamas, I clearly remember thinking, *Well, would you look at that.* Suddenly a little lightbulb came on inside my head, and within ten years ninety percent of my work was coming directly from the Internet.

As the years rolled by, I also unexpectedly began to gather a bit of notoriety among other carvers who had been following my magazine articles, and some of them started showing up at my doorstep. Two guys I had been hearing about for some time were the Boni Brothers. Rick and Randy were identical twins, massively talented artists, and had quite a unique life story as well. Both were born with severe cataracts and were legally blind until their mid-twenties, when they were among the very first people to receive the newly developed corrective surgery. We became close friends almost immediately and they would go on to start the famous Ridgway Chainsaw Carvers Rendezvous, of which I'll say more about later.

It was this encounter, however, that presented me with another opportunity to use my newfound Internet skills when I realized the need for a better way to connect this new and rapidly forming carving community. There was a company in California that had just developed Internet forums, which was the forerunner of today's modern platforms like Facebook, and with that I started the "Carving Post." It immediately became very popular and was averaging between ten to twenty thousand hits a day, which was astronomical back then.

There were people from almost forty countries participating, so the humble little Pine Hollow Studio truly was taking its place as the new "World Headquarters."

The studio with my 'festival rig' which unfortunately burned-up in a fire late one night on the way home from a show in Virginia. (I'll say more about this later) What you cannot see in this photo is the shop is painted bright yellow with green vines growing up the sides, and eventually covering the entire building like a little Hobbit house. It was a charming place and drew allot of attention from passerby's.

In "Full Cossack" with Nelli at a local Chuvash museum.
Kazakh and Mongol regions very much overlap with the
Slav's (which includes both Russia and Ukraine), and have
similar garb. I've heard estimates that upwards of one in
eight people in this part of the world have traces of
Genghis Kahn DNA.

Five

Russian Roots …

It was my parent's fifty-year anniversary party at the Mountain View Inn and a big winter storm had settled in, so we were all surprised by how many people actually made it that night. Partway into the evening, my dad decided to have our first father-son talk out in the parking lot. I was forty-nine at the time, but better late than never, I suppose. He had two points to make: First, we need to stop with all the Pollock jokes around Mom, which I instantly translated into it being him who was in trouble and he must have recently caught hell about that.

I should explain that my mother is 100 percent American-born Polish, and her brothers, whom I very much love, had incessantly made Pollock jokes for as long as I could remember. Ethnic jokes were still in fashion back then and they had one for every occasion; you couldn't get through lunch without three or four getting passed around, and it did, of course, rub off on some of us younger ones.

The second point Dad had to make, turned him more serious. He looked me straight in the eye and said, "Your great grandfather was a Russian Jew." I'm not sure, maybe he thought that was devastating news, and it was hard to hide my amusement, thinking he was about to tell me they were changing their last name, moving back to Poland, or some such other earth-shattering news.

I said, "Thanks for telling me all that Dad; it's freezing out here, let's go back inside."

The first chance I had to meet some "real Russians" came when my youngest son was chosen to play on a little all-star soccer team for an international tournament hosted by the Sister Cities foundation. By this point in time, Pittsburgh was no longer a steel-producing city, but nevertheless we were matched up with Novokuznetsk, Russia, which probably wasn't in the steel business any longer either. Part of this included hosting the visiting team(s) and bringing them with us for the weeklong event held in Louisville, Kentucky.

Keep in mind this was around 1990 and just after the collapse of the Soviet Union when international travel between our two countries was beginning to open up. The Russian team was made up of two groups, one under twelve in age, and the other under sixteen, plus a small entourage including a coach. (Yes, only one coach for two all-boy soccer teams). Also included were a few of their financial sponsors, and one translator, which was lucky because we had absolutely none. It was around sixty people in all and right from the beginning, I realized many of them, the kids especially, had never been more than a hundred kilometers from their home in Siberia. Now they were halfway around the world, and in a country that for many years they must have heard mostly bad things about.

It was only later on that we began to realize what a brave and incredible journey it must have been for them. First a four-day train ride to Moscow, then the long overnight flight to America, a day or two of sightseeing in Washington, DC, then a bus ride to Pittsburgh before another day-long drive to Louisville.

There were probably only a few people in their group who had any idea what the event might involve, while everybody else was just along for the crazy adventure. I cannot even begin to imagine what it must have been like for the families back home to send their kids off for a month-long trip into the great unknown.

The Sisters City tournament included around sixty countries. We all stayed in the same high-rise hotel, the Gault House, in Louisville, and pretty much took over the place. Tables, chairs, and any and everything else in the big conference rooms were immediately pushed into the corners to make room for indoor scrimmaging. Any and all food services were soon emptied as well, and there was an incredible buzz of energy like I had never before experienced at a sport related event.

We soon came to discover that our little entourage were among the lucky ones who were assigned rooms on lower floors and could use the stairway. This was a twenty-five-floor hotel and even from the eighth floor it was much faster to walk up or down, as opposed to waiting for an elevator. They were in constant use and could include a long wait, and were already packed beyond capacity when it finally did arrive.

Did you know that elevators have an over-weight alarm buzzer? It's true. The kids would pile in on top of each other and just when you thought it had reached the limit, four more would somehow squeeze in. The only thing stopping this mayhem was the loud buzzer.

Almost immediately the group split in half between the young and older ones for day-to-day activities, and we were responsible for the younger ones.

Another friend and I both had big custom-size travel vans that could manage all of our group of around twenty or so people, and we soon learned about their two new favorite American things: McDonald's and grocery stores. We would hit both places at least once a day and soon discovered what the grocery store attraction was about – the fresh fruit section. They had never seen, or could imagine anything like it, and I personally filled two boxes per day for them.

My friend who had the other big van told the kids his name was "Good-looking Guy," which was always amusing with their little Russian accents, and it was also funny to see the reaction from other shoppers when one of them would call out, "Hey, Good-looking Guy, buy more apples!"

They were a well-behaved bunch in general so we always gave them some leeway to explore, and one time I came around the corner of a frozen food aisle and noticed some people standing back as though watching something. There was a big bin of rubber beach balls on sale, and the kids had found it and a spontaneous scrimmage had broken out. I hid back for a minute or two and just watched in amazement; their skills were quite good and they were passing really well, and I noticed some other shoppers who might normally be put off by a soccer match in the frozen food aisle seemed to be enjoying it too. It was actually a wonderful sight as I realized those kids felt safe, and were making the most of every minute. They probably wouldn't have been any happier even in Disneyland at that moment.

Our last night was memorable as well. We unexpectedly met up with Sergei, the Russian coach, and finally had a chance to spend some time with him. Up to that time he had been pretty much unapproachable, plus he didn't look very friendly, but we soon discovered why: he was the single person responsible for the safety (and success) of both teams. His charge was forty wild and young little scrappers in the competition of their young lives. Plus if that wasn't enough, they were all representing their country, the Motherland. It's hard to imagine, let alone put into words, the amount of raw energy, passion, and emotions involved.

And poor Sergei. Think about it for a minute, and it should be no big surprise that he didn't smile much. He spoke not a single word of English, was twelve time zones away from home, and was now in a strange place he probably couldn't even pronounce. On this last night, however, he finally let his guard down a bit and was comfortable enough to come out and have some time off, so we dragged him up to the rooftop café for some good, clean, adult fun. Communication was slow at first, but eventually we pieced together that they had been away from home for over three weeks already, traveling to strange and unknown places, and nobody back home so far had heard a single word from them. I couldn't imagine how it would feel with the situation reversed and what must have been going through all of their minds. Multiply forty kids by the parents, grandparents, friends, teachers, and probably an extended support group, which translated into hundreds of worried people holding their breath. Very brave indeed, on both sides.

Just then I noticed a pay phone over in the corner and grabbed Sergei by the arm while pointing to the phone, then pulled out my credit card and we got started. This was a good decade before cell phones so it took a little while, but eventually we found an international operator that connected us with another operator, and finally a Russian operator who finally got him through to his wife. I could tell his excitement instantly by his face. "Tatiana!" Then a minute later his face went blank, he lost the call so we started over again and this time he was able to have a good, long conversation.

I wandered back to our table while they talked and tried to imagine how many phone lines would be lighting up all over Novokuznetsk in a couple minutes. Sergei finished the call, charged back over to the table and I got the biggest hug of my life. That was truly one of the highlights of the entire experience.

It was getting pretty late by then and since we were all leaving in the morning we said our farewells and headed outside the hotel for some fresh air. Suddenly, a taxi pulled up and out came two of the sponsors whom we hadn't really met so far, but were very curious about. I was with two of our coaches and we watched in amusement as they tumbled out of the taxi loaded up with a bundle of packages and said goodbye to some girls in the cab. One of the businessmen instantly spotted us, and next thing I knew we were following them up to their room for a last night toast. It turned out they were curious about us as well, so we had a little party.

One guy quickly pushed everything aside except for a little table, pulled up five chairs, and then out came the biggest switchblade knife I'd ever seen.

These guys were certainly drunk at this point, but you have to realize, we were too. The other guy pulled out a giant Snickers bar, which is what the knife was for (to our great relief), cut it into five neat little pieces, then out came the vodka. Of course we had no translator at this time but eventually it didn't seem to matter; things became much easier after we stumbled onto the subject of fishing. From there on the only other memory I have from that night is quite possibly the worst hangover of my life. In the top ten for sure…

And just a quick follow up for our soccer fans here on how the tournament shook-out. Sixty countries, as mentioned, and our Pittsburgh team was properly destroyed early on. The Russians made it a bit further, and I believe it was Sheffield, England, who took first in the end. (Another ex-steel producing city, go figure.)

Not long after that I had a carving project for a family who owned a summer home on the Allegheny River in Pennsylvania, just a few hours' drive from home. The customer and I had communicated ahead of time about ideas, where and how to find the house, and set a date. This was before GPS navigational devices were available, so specific directions were always helpful and sometimes included details like "when you get closer, start looking for an old dump truck on the right, then turn left, we're at the end of the lane, you can't miss it." I knew it was a silly question, but I had to ask anyhow: "What if they move the dump truck?" She said not to worry, the dump truck hadn't moved for twenty years, and I found the place without any problems.

We both arrived around the same time and she pulled up in a big summer camp-type van. The door slid open and out charged five excited little blonde-haired kids, and one big Irish setter. Next came the mom, a nice-looking lady with a young baby cradled in her arms, and we all moved over to the big river view porch for snacks and introductions. The kids looked through my books while the mom and I talked about some different carving ideas and finally agreed on one, so I headed back over to the van to get prepared for the day. The dog and five little blonde kids followed me over and it was great; they were all funny and well-behaved, though a bit shy at first, but that didn't last for long.

While I was putting on my work boots, one of the boys began to explore my van and soon found my squirt gun collection, and don't judge me here but, yes, some of them were loaded. You can probably guess what happened next: a full-on battle broke out. Before long one of the boys squirted their dog in the face (which he very much didn't like) and the girls started to yell at him in Russian. This caught my attention, of course, so I said to the mom: "Ma'am, the kids are speaking Russian here." She laughed, sat down with the baby, and told me their story.

Several years prior she and her husband had traveled to Russia to adopt a child. It was through an agency and they were hoping for a girl. On the day after arriving they had traveled to an orphanage where they met and spent some time with various kids before they made a final decision. There was one little girl they both instantly fell in love with and just felt like it was meant to be, only there was one little problem. The officials went on to explain that the little girl had four other siblings, five in all.

They all had the same mother, but the fathers were unknown, so they were trying to keep them all together. So they returned to the hotel that night, partially devastated, and she told me, "You can't imagine what a night it was. We prayed and cried, prayed some more, didn't sleep much, of course, then returned the next day and adopted all five." Around a year later the adoption agency called and said that the same woman had had another baby, and asked if they wanted to adopt her too. I was looking down at the small child in her arms while she finished the story. She added, "People always talk about life-changing moments, but I could have never imagined anything like this."

With the six adopted siblings. This photo was taken over twenty years ago, so they would all be close to thirty now.

It was a ten-hour flight from New York to Moscow, a bit long and somewhat boring, but not always. Sometimes on the return flight I noticed people traveling with newly adopted kids, and it was hard not to notice what a traumatic experience it must have been for the child. Some of the older ones were fairly calm, but the younger ones quite often had a difficult time, and it must have been more than a little challenging for the new parents, so I developed a little rescue act.

I would pretend to be just passing by and stop unexpectedly, kneel down and say, "*Privet, kokdilla, marlinky?*" (Hi, how are you, little one?) in as friendly tone as possible, to get their attention. After a wink to the parents, I would take out the *Sky Miles* magazine from their seat folder, tear some pages out, then slowly start folding them into small paper airplanes. Then I would sail one down the aisle while making the *shroooom* sound like a real airplane. This always got a smile from the little one.

Keep in mind that some of these kids had possibly ridden in a car before, but probably never a train, and certainly never an enormous airplane that was going to the other side of the world. It must have felt like going to the moon for some of them. So my little rescue act worked every time, and pretty soon paper airplanes were flying around all over the place with other people joining in sometimes. See – those silly magazines really were good for something.

Another interesting thing I observed on these flights was that some of the kids had obvious physical or emotional issues, things you maybe wouldn't notice at a glance except with an eye for it. But the new foster parents were completely aware and accepting of it.

My little paper airplane stops almost always ended in a short conversation with the new mom and dad. One time in particular stands out where I couldn't guess the boy's age, but could clearly see the absolute terror in his eyes. So I got busy making some new airplanes and going through my little practiced greeting, and finally got him to soften up a bit. I wanted to ask the mom about his medical conditions, but in the end I just said what a beautiful child he was, and tears of joy started running down her face. Seldom in life do we have a chance to experience such pure instant love and happiness.

A little side note that relates to this story: There was an orphanage in Cheboksary we visited a few times, and there was a little girl who stood out from all the other wonderful smiling faces. We even briefly considered bringing her with us, so I totally understood the connection that many others felt. Later on the director shared this girl's history: she had a brother living there as well, they were both HIV positive (from birth), but doing well, and they were already spoken for and moving to California very soon.

In more recent years I discovered that the entire foster and adoption system in Russia had undergone fundamental changes and the smaller local orphanages I'd visited had been absorbed into different parts of temporary-care facilities and placement programs. The same thing happened in America decades ago with government funding (along with extensive involvement from the Catholic diocese) and hasn't existed for some time.

I'll always be thankful to have been around to experience and share the end of such an interesting era that most people know very little about.

At the orphanage in Cheboksary which I visited a few times. One time I brought a box of frisbees and that was a huge hit.

I've traveled to Russia eight times to date, and along the way have had many opportunities to visit schools and culture centers in and around Cheboksary. This would include elementary grades up to, and including, university level.

On occasion, I demonstrated my carving outside in a schoolyard, but most of the time it was simply an indoor PowerPoint presentation with a translator stuck to my side. The excitement was always incredible, especially among the younger students. They would crowd around me afterward and move in any direction I moved, like a school of little fish. Eventually a teacher would bark at them to make some room, but it didn't last long; very soon I would be swarmed again and signing autographs by the hundreds.

I should mention that the teachers had a great interest as well, and almost always invited us to lunch or dinner of some kind – they were wonderful people. I realized that often times I was the first American that many of them had met. Older staff members could be a bit reserved at first, but that would soon melt away and for the most part the teachers and local volunteers embraced me without reservation.

The kids, however, were always predictable in their over-the-top excitement. I would always bring in a backpack of photo albums to show and had just enough self-confidence to speak in front of a room full of strangers. Strangely enough, doing that in a foreign country seemed easier than back at home and I would eventually come to learn something very important about Russian culture: They speak from the heart first, and brain second.

Dedication ceremony at the 'Park of Five Hundred Years'. It was two days of visitors from all over the city and many musical performances by school children.

Traditional Chuvash outfit.

This photo was taken the last time I saw Mr. Palmer. It was a dedication ceremony at Indian Lake Golf Course in Pennsylvania, the very first of hundreds he would eventually design over the course of his great career.

Six

Mulligan ...

Kathleen Palmer contacted me out of the clear blue one day and said that little Mulligan, Arnie's beloved dog, had passed away. She asked me if I could possibly make a small memorial piece for them. Of course I was happy to, but didn't realize at the time it would include the burial ceremony as well.

Without question, the highlight of my carving career was the work I did for the Palmer family of Latrobe, Pennsylvania. The very first project was carving a likeness of their father, Deke, into a pine stump that father and son had planted together fifty years prior.

I already knew he was very famous in the golf world but not being raised in a golfing-type family myself, I really had no idea what a legend he was on other fronts as well. Of course I was a bit nervous. What I've come to appreciate in recent years is how so many famous people turn out to be extremely personable in normal life as well, and that was certainly the case here. On our first meeting, he grabbed my hand and thanked me for coming over, then explained how the grounds crew was cutting the tree down but had left this big stump so a machine could push it over. He happened to be passing through that morning and stopped the guys, saying, "Hey, wait a minute, Dad and I planted this tree together, so why don't we find one of those guys to carve a statue?"

Up until that point I had no idea what they might want and asked, "What are you thinking about here?" He replied, "We'd like a statue of Dad here, can you do that?" This happened very early in my carving career, but I so clearly remember that moment like it was yesterday. It was one of those moments when time speeds up and slows down at the same time, and I began slowly shaking my head up and down, searching for the right words. Actually there were only two words possible, yes or no, and through a process of elimination, I realized "no" would mean go home and probably regret it for the rest of my life. "Yes, I think I can do that," finally came out. He smiled, slapped me on the shoulder and said: "I know you can!"

It took a full week to complete and I'm hard-pressed to point a finger to another carving project so challenging and unique. They had given me the old attic box filled with personal family photos for reference, things like him teaching little Arnie how to play golf, and many other very personal and nostalgic items. I felt like a museum curator holding on to them for a few days. Sometimes on a break I would wander over to the clubhouse, or business office, and find so many incredible photos from his life and career. For example: sitting on a couch with Queen Elizabeth, having lunch with Tiger Woods and Bill Clinton, George and Barbara Bush, and other former presidents. Looking back I realize he had given me full access to everything possible to a good job on "Pap."

The best part, however, was the personal one-on-one conversations we had. He was so friendly, interesting, and inspiring. His normal daily routine at home would include playing through the course twice a day, once in the early morning and then once in the late afternoon, but he always made time to come over and see how it was going.

"Now remember," he would explain, "Dad had a pretty serious face most of the time, but if you knew him well enough he always had a little upturned smile in the back, but you had to look real close."

Around the second or third day some people from the office came by and said, "We're going to plan a photo shoot of the carving in progress with you and Mr. Palmer tomorrow."

Coincidently I actually had something else planned for that exact date, which had been planned for a long time. Along with a few other artist friends, we had planned a daylong art/career event at a teen rehabilitation center near Pittsburgh and there was absolutely no way I could have backed out. It was a little awkward until Mr. Palmer, who happened to be listening nearby while I was apologizing, came over with a big smile and another friendly slap on the shoulder.

A short time after that I wrote a story about this experience for my *Chip Chats* magazine column, which I had to send to his office for permission before publication. Two days later they sent it back with permission and included two little correction notes handwritten by Mr. Palmer, and I was a little more than relieved because the story had a twist that I wasn't sure he would like.

My story was primarily centered around the dad, and the challenge of creating a statue of someone long since passed away through photos and personal stories about their life. I had chosen not to mention Arnie by name. Instead, I described Deke as he was: A hardworking and determined man who had raised a family, built a golf course, and taught his famous son how to play. I closed the article with the following: "I found extra confidence in myself just thinking about all he had accomplished in his life and hoped he would be satisfied with my work."

Another thing happened around the same time. I was talking to Mrs. Palmer one day (it was Winnie at this time) and somehow the subject of books came up, probably related to flying, and I happened to mention that I had just finished Chuck Yeager's second personal biography. She didn't know about that book yet but assured me that she would find it soon.

"Arnie and Chuck are friends, you know," she said, and he's in the final stage of writing his own autobiography as well, on the last chapter I think." A short time later *A Golfer's Life* came into publication and I'm going to include here the very last page. Sometimes I wonder if our words mixed near the end and maybe I was a small part of that.

As I stated at the outset of this reflection, autumn's arrival in western Pennsylvania always fills me with a bittersweet pleasure; it means soon we'll be headed to the warmth of Bay Hill, but it also announces that another golf season back home has come and gone.

Lacking the gift of prophecy, I can't tell you how many more times I'll get to go around that old golf course before I join my parents on the hilltop near the 18th green. But I can promise you that going around it never fails to delight and surprise me, and on this particular Indian summer day, our first day back since the start of Winnie's medical treatment, I was walking up the 18th fairway when I saw him.

He was standing just off the fairway about three hundred yards out from the tee, where only a few weeks before a tall and regal pine had stood. That tree was very special to me. I can remember as if it was yesterday the day my father and I planted it. I was about six years old and was allowed to ride on the root ball of the young tree as we hauled it to the freshly dug hole beside the 18th fairway in the back of our old ford truck.

The tree, which was roughly the same age as me, had grown nearly seventy five feet tall and lived a good life. But now it had died a natural death of old age, and I hated to say goodbye to it. In fact I commented to my brother, Jerry, that I wished we could find some fitting way to memorialize it – maybe carve a statue out of its stump or something. A few days later Jerry found a talented wood carver who worked with chainsaws, and the result of his artistry was now standing ten feet high on the side of the fairway with his hands on his hips, staring up the hill at the 18th green.

It was unmistakably Pap, keeping a sharp eye out for anybody who was foolish enough not to fix his divot or properly repair his ball mark on the green.

I stood there looking up at him for the longest time, deeply moved to have him back, pleasantly lost in my own thoughts, vaguely aware of the high school band practicing for the big homecoming game that weekend just across the valley from the golf course, wondering what my Pap would make of this golfers life. Some things never change. I still hope he'd be pleased.

A few summers before he passed away was around the time that Mrs. Palmer (Kathleen) contacted me about the memorial plaque for little Mulligan. She had a sketch, very simple but nice, and also shared some stories about how much Arnie loved him. Apparently the little guy had multiple issues, and had gone through fifteen or so operations over the years, including jaw restoration and various other major problems. She also said he went everywhere with them and he even had his own seat on the floor of their plane, right between the pilot seats. Although Mr. Palmer was a great pilot for most of his life, he wasn't flying in the right seat anymore, but could still be found in the left fairly often. (Keep in mind, it's a big plane.) So I suppose it wasn't such a bad dog's life.

For the memorial piece, we made arrangements ahead of time for me to go over, meet someone from the office for final placement details, and install it as a surprise while they were away. Their house was very close to the office, just a short walking distance actually, and the final instructions were pretty simple: To put it two feet back from the corner, a certain height off the ground.

Then he handed me a little bag and I asked "What's this?" I was a little surprised when he replied, "Well, it's Mulligan, of course." There was a small decorative wooden box with his ashes inside, so I had to dig the hole deeper and say a little prayer before placing him under the memorial. Yes, I buried Arnold Palmer's dog and how many people can say that? But seriously, I don't mean to make light of a personal loss like that and was quite humbled to be asked in the first place.

To date, I have also carved four life-size statues of Arnie in full swing for different golf resorts that he designed, and each time they had an unveiling ceremony connected with the new course grand opening. It was expected that I be on hand and it did get a bit easier after a while, but that very first time was quite an intense experience. Hundreds of people were milling around, anxiously waiting for the ceremony to begin, plus it was around ninety degrees in the shade and I was already sweating bullets, hoping he would like it.

Sitting back in the crowd, I had time to think about the exact moment he would first see it, and what his reaction would be. A smile, a frown, maybe nothing? Actually by this time I already knew him well enough to realize he was far too much of a gentleman to show any kind of negative expression, so through a process of simple deduction I realized it would be a smile or nothing, the latter meaning he didn't like it. In situations like that you have just enough time to realize it was going to be a big life moment.

Well, to cut through all the suspense, his reaction was amazing and unlike anything I could imagine. He instantly got a really big, smile on his face, then turned toward the crowd to find me and gave a big "come on up" wave.

The fourth and last ceremony was pretty amazing, too. It was a rededication to a course he had designed early in his career; it was Indian Lake (Pennsylvania) and it turned out it was his very first one. Prior to the event, I had mentioned to somebody on the Indian Lake staff that, "One of these days it sure would be great to have a photo of him and me together."

By then I had observed literally hundreds of photo situations with him and fans, and saw how much he still enjoyed it, which was yet another amazing facet of his personality. In fact, this was very much a part of his popularity and overall legend, as well. At the beginning of the dedication, the usually large enthusiastic group of fans was on hand, waiting for him to arrive, and I was hanging back in the crowd trying hard to look casual. Eventually a little entourage of golf carts appeared over the hill and the place went ecstatic, as usual. With him were some people from the office I already knew, plus several close family members, that made a fair-size group all in all.

What happened next was another surreal moment. Mr. Palmer stepped out of his cart, shook a few hands, then swung his head around and said, "Where's Joe?" Apparently word of my wish for a photo together had gotten back to him, and what an amazing day it was that followed.

There was a big area cordoned-off area with a ribbon holding the crowd at bay, plus hundreds of cameras snapping away while he and I walked around, talking like we were the only two people there.

Sometimes a friend will ask me what it was like to meet him in person, and here is what I normally say, word for word: "He has such a presence about him that say, for example, you were from another planet and didn't know anything about anything, you could easily tell he was someone very special."

After getting to know him a little bit, it's even more amazing what a special person he really was. I am astounded how someone with so much talent and success could be so humble and still enjoy personal contact with ordinary people like me. Plus I finally got my photo, quite a few actually, and they are all wonderful, but pale in comparison to the memory of spending a little time together. We should all be so lucky to have a such an experience like that.

Chip Chats has been in publication for 68 years and is one of the longest running and most well- established woodcarving magazines ever produced. Prior to this photo being taken, I had been a regular contributor for quite a number of years, writing in a column entitled: "Reflections of a Chainsaw Sculptor," which is also the sub-title of this book. And what an honor to have the first ever chainsaw carving make the cover.

Seven

Mount Nebo ...

Uncle Jeff called one morning. He was working as a realtor at the time in the Laurel Highlands where I had been looking for a new place to live, and said that two more properties just came across his desk, so to come on up.

It's a wonderful area with ski resorts, state parks, whitewater rafting, and possibly the nicest rail trail system in this part of the country. Best of all, everything is within an hour's drive of Pittsburgh, so naturally we fell in love with this place a long time ago. I hurried on up the following day and once again reminded Jeff of the rules before we started out, simple: 1) no barking dogs. It was a motivating factor for wanting to move in the first place, so I wasn't even getting out of the car if I heard barking, and 2) there had to be a house. I had built quite a number of them in my earlier years but it was a lot of work, plus I didn't think I could even afford to do that and for sure didn't want to start from scratch.

So off we went to see the first place. It looked pretty good from a distance, but as we got closer I started to hear barking and not just a little bit. It was kind of bizarre actually, that on these large mountain lots somebody had put their dog kennel right on the property line and quite close to the house we'd come to see. I put my window up and turned the radio on. Jeff frowned and said, "All right, all right," but was not the least bit discouraged.

So we started out for the second property, which wasn't very far from the first one, just a little higher up the mountain. As we got closer it started to take on a nice private feeling, more so than any place we'd looked at before, and not a dog in sight. Pretty soon he stopped the car on the little mountainside road, looked around and said, "Okay, this is it!" He then jumped out of the car and started looking for a property line or landmark, and said, "Has to be right around here somewhere."

And I said, "Nice property, Jeff, but where's the house?"

I got out to have a quick look around anyhow, Mr. Skeptical, but Jeff was very excited and went straight into a sermon about not letting little details like "no house" hold me back. It was, however, very quiet and secluded which I instantly liked, but the property was a big mess and difficult to even walk through. It was a real forest, covered with big old-growth trees of many different species, but some had fallen here and there and were now covered with brush and thorn bushes. Soon however, we found a deer trail and were able to make our way up to the ridgeline to get a feel for the overall size from where he thought was the upper property line. Neither one of us had any idea what five wooded acres was supposed to look like, but from there to the road looked pretty big, so it made sense. But there was a catch: He also explained that there was a waiting list for parcels around this size, so I had to let him know by the next Monday. It was already Friday, so I said, "Never mind, just go ahead and call somebody else who can deal with this mess."

Jeff laughed, gave me a big hug and said, "Okay, I have to get on with my day now, but I'll wait for your call." We grabbed a quick lunch together and afterward I grabbed a six-pack and drove back over for one last look.

Picking my way back to the ridge I sat there for a while, relaxing in the quiet shade, and a thought slowly crept into my mind: *There is no way on God's green earth I want to get into this much work.*

The next day I called Jeff and said to go ahead and get the papers ready- I'm in. One day a few weeks later I drove up to meet the surveyors who were there marking property lines, it was the day before our final closing and something funny happened. Keep in mind, there was no driveway access at this time, so everybody had to park on the road, and although their truck was already there, they were nowhere to be found. So I headed up to the now-familiar ridgeline but still couldn't find them so I hollered out, "Hello, hello," and was confused when they finally answered back quite a distance from where I thought they should be. Slowly picking my way over I eventually found them and asked, "Hey guys, what the heck are you doing way over here?" One of them smiled and said, "What the heck do you think we're doing way over here?" Suddenly I realized our mistake—my mistake actually—the ridgeline wasn't the back side of the property; it was the middle, so this parcel turned out to be exactly twice as big as we had thought in the beginning. It was kind of like when you order a small salad and they accidently bring the large deluxe, only a thousand times better.

The following day we signed all the papers and suddenly realized it was December seventh, and once again I found myself in an attorney's office on the very same date I had signed for my studio property so many years earlier. Of course Uncle Jeff was there for the occasion, and I need to add a couple notes about that.

He's not really an uncle, as you may have already guessed. It's always been a traditional code word or title between close friends when you have young children, a nice and endearing way to forego formalities like "Mr. Wilson," or "Mr. King," and so forth. It's much more casual, and I'm still "Uncle Joe" in Jeff's family.

The other thing I need to mention here is that Jeff also happens to be the most prolific musician I've ever had the pleasure to personally endure. He is a guy who can stand up in front of two, or two hundred people, sing his heart out and bring the room down, as they say. This is something I have personally observed many times. Beyond that, he is also one of the most kind and spiritual souls who has passed through my life and was helpful at some other important junctures as well. Seriously, I think he is the one who should be writing a book...

Change can be hard for some, even a bit scary and I experienced both emotions when it came time to build the house. My biggest fear at the time was that my life would start changing so fast and I could never go back to this safe and cozy little space that I had carved out for myself, and then it would keep on changing forever. (This is what actually happened) During the last few weeks before moving out of my old house I would sometimes wake up in the middle of the night, pull the covers up over my head and think, *Man, what are you doing?*

But this trepidation was short-lived; two days after moving into the summer/construction camp, all that was behind me forever, and what a wonderful release it was. I remember a quote from an old friend; "any risk you take in life that doesn't scare the shit out of you isn't worth it."

We spent the first few years sleeping in a primitive little campsite we made up on the ridge, with just a tent, a campfire, and sometimes a new grandson.

Two close friends agreed to help with the initial building process. One was my faithful shop helper and best buddy, Mike, who lived kind-of nearby, and the other was Pablo, who lived in Canada. Pablo was actually a nickname we hung on him as he and his wife would winter in Mexico every year. He was fluent in Spanish and loved the culture, but was actually born and raised in Switzerland, and now married to a lovely French girl, and was living on Prince Edward Island in Canada. Pablo also had a very organized and meticulous side, plus a natural born genius at fixing things.

One night he told us a story about the time they were crossing the Sahara Desert in a Land Rover, and halfway through the fuel pump broke. It took him almost two days, but he was finally able to file down a little piece of metal from nail clippers and make the repair. This story came along one night right after we finally got electricity and phone service, but somebody left the phone unit out in the rain (it might have been me). Mike and I watched in amazement while he completely disassembled it, laid all the tiny little inside pieces on rocks around the campfire to dry out, then casually put it all back together again. It still didn't work but we had great fun watching him in action.

Only later did I realize how it must have made him a bit crazy that we were building a house without blueprints. A year before construction started I began to make drawings and little cardboard models based on design ideas that might work with the slightly sloped terrain. After a year of countless ideas, it started to make *me* crazy trying to decide which one to go with, so I finally threw them all away and pulled something off the top of my head the day before we started. And no blueprint.

On the last day of major framing, we were finishing up the roof and there was one little piece of plywood with a complicated shape, so rather than try to holler down the dimensions I just sketched it on a small cardboard and dropped it down to where him and Mike were cutting things. He probably thought I couldn't hear him as he growled in his thick Swiss accent: "First goddam blueprint I see since I been here."

The three of us did well together. We were up early each morning, building the house during the day, and then finally were able to gather around the campfire each night for dinner. Sometimes we would start happy hour while drying out our clothes around the hot flames, get some food cooking, and sometimes even a little guitar playing if it wasn't raining. Slowly but surely, things began to take shape and eventually she was completely under roof, but I still had a long way to go when my buddies had to say farewell. I could never have come this far without them.

A funny side note to this part of the story; Pablo's real name is Kurt, and a short time later he and Lorraine built a house as well. They have beautiful ocean front property on the island and on my very first visit I couldn't wait to ask about their blueprints. To my utter amazement, he eventually fessed-up that they didn't need them and just kind of winged-it. And it's beautiful, "Muy buen Pablo de la montaña!"

So from then on after my buddies left the work days went from ten to fourteen hours, but it really wasn't so bad, that is until winter came. I was still camping out but did have some heat in the trailer-

-but no more campfires. Pretty much everything outside was frozen solid which was a good incentive to keep moving, and by somewhere in the middle of December I was finally able to sleep indoors again. It was far from finished, however, the proverbial "work in progress." A year prior to starting I had taken out several large hard wood trees (oak, cherry, and some others) to have them kiln dried and milled for all the interior finishing. This part took quite a bit longer than I had hoped for, but it also turned out way nicer than I had expected, and although I have no regrets about that, I'll probably never do it again…

Under construction, August 2003. I took almost a year off from work in order to do this.

Sometimes people comment about how cool it must have been to do something like that on your own. But honestly? It all felt very natural at the time, almost expected in a strange kind of way and now that I've been living here for this long it feels like slipping on a comfortable old sweater, or favorite slippers in the morning. It's where I'm supposed to be, and what a blessing this place found me.

It would be fun to add a few words about the little mountain town close to where we live; Two stop signs, a post office, fruit & vegetable market, butcher shop, some seasonal gift shops, and three general convenience-type stores. Star Market is the most popular because it also has gas pumps and a restaurant, and somewhat of a community nerve center like in an old movie.

One day I went inside to pay for gas and there was a plastic jar beside the cash register with a simple note asking for donations. It read: "Please help with a funeral expense." The girl working there said it was for her cousin. They had a boy who was born with a terrible brain deformity and was not expected to survive, but lived for twelve years. He had just passed away and the family was completely bottomed out, emotionally as well as financially. It was not the first time I'd seen a jar beside the register, and I always throw something in, but this time a little light bulb lit up inside my brain.

I asked her to find the owner, Keith. He's a big guy, kind of jovial, and always friendly to me, like most people from the community I've come to know.

Friendly is as far as you'll ever get around here. Not that I ever look for anything else; it's just an observation, and not at all uncommon in smaller communities around the world. At the time, Keith already knew that I was a carver, but I have to back up a bit and explain why. I forgot to mention that there are also over ten sawmills within a five-mile radius of this little town, which might seem like a lot but as I understand that's way less than not so long ago.

So anyhow, I'd done business at some of these mills. Keith had a log truck and probably went to high school with most of the mill owners, so on any given day, you'd see various other log trucks coming and going from the market. I soon came to understand that there are very few secrets within this side of the community, and it was a safe bet he that already knew more about me than I realized.

So I told him my idea: I had a little bear carving somebody had ordered and didn't pick up (the second part was a lie). I told him I could bring it down with a roll of raffle tickets and the girls up in the restaurant could take it from there. Close your eyes for a moment and imagine a spunky little waitress, like from another scene in an old movie, working in a place filled with of odd-looking regulars. The cook scurries in and out of the kitchen to say hi to somebody, everybody knows everybody and eventually you discover that many of them are related as well. Martha was the unspoken queen bee however, and had probably been here the longest. She is an absolute bundle of energy with the natural glow of someone who really enjoys what they were doing, loved the idea and could get a lot of mileage out of this, so Keith agreed.

Right away he promised to put my cards beside it and maybe find some business for me, but I stopped him right there and explained that I wanted no part of that, and wanted to remain completely anonymous. I didn't want people looking at me funny every time I went in there, to which he was amused and started to chuckle; "Well, it's a little late for that, Joe."

The raffle ticket idea went pretty well as I had hoped, and sometime later I got a handwritten thank you note in the mail. I'm not sure who it was from but it was very nice and unexpected. But something else even more unexpected changed after that. Some people still look at me kind of funny from time to time, but the people working there treat me differently now, or *not* differently might be a better description. I was no longer a transplant or a stranger, just another customer, and that has advantages.

One day in the restaurant I had an old-knitted ski hat on that someone made for me a long time ago. It wasn't my favorite, but had "Joe King" cleverly crocheted on the front, and Martha clucked at me with obvious disapproval: "Where'd you get that hat?" she asked. I explained that it was from an old girlfriend, but that we already broken up. "Good," she clucked, "what can I get you, hon?" At the bottom of our hill is a lovely little "rail trail" that meanders through the valley and follows what they call Indian Creek, although it's more like a small river at times. We are avid hikers here, plus we have a big crazy dog that loves to run, so we use it almost every day.

Most of this type of trail system in and around

Pennsylvania has replaced abandoned railways, which tended to follow the rivers and creeks, allowing for the logistical practicality of steady, gradual descending grades that were best suited for trains.

These surrounding mountainous areas are also abundant in natural recourses, coal and timber in particular, which very much helped fuel the industrial revolution in America. Pittsburgh was an epicenter for these blossoming industries, which were greatly accelerated by the world wars when demand for steel, iron and other metals met an all-time high. Eventually, however, the markets changed and demand dropped off substantially after World War II, and the rail systems connecting the supply line were mothballed almost overnight. After some years went by and it became apparent it was never coming back, some entrepreneurial individuals discovered a market for the rusty old rails and began harvesting them for the scrap metal business. They were followed by newly forming groups of "hike & bike" enthusiasts, who collectively began improving the old rail beds and eventually created the extensive system of interconnecting recreational trail systems we now enjoy. It's also interesting to note that during the time the trains were running, there was almost no passenger service. It was simply a raw materials link, and how ironic that those same paths are now used solely for recreation.   For example, our little trail now connects to one a ways down the valley, which then connects to another bigger one, and at this juncture we could turn right and end up in Pittsburgh (after 50 miles or so).

Or we could hang a left and follow it all the way to Washington, DC (around 175 miles). What an amazing transformation; recycling abandoned leftovers from a long-ago and almost forgotten era of such industrial fortitude. I think most people using the trails today never give a second thought to any of the historical value. For the most part, I think people simply enjoy the opportunity for such nearby and wonderful places to get outdoors, walk the crazy dog, and let our minds drift off for a while. I have also, on occasion, let my imagination wonder about what it must have been like for all the hardworking people who originally built the infrastructure. I think about all that back-breaking work with long hours and small pay, and I wonder if any of their off-spring realizes, or are even aware of, the legacy they left behind.

Draper- our big crazy Doberman. He thinks it's his trail and everybody comes here to see him.

Eight

Left Coasters ...

The great Pacific Northwest coast is about as an unforgettable and amazing place as you're likely to ever find. Vast areas of cascading mountain chains falling into jagged weather-beaten coastlines with rivers and streams racing toward the boiling surf below for hundreds of miles in all directions. It's truly something you have to see in person to realize the enormous scale, and feel the sea-battered coastline crashing and rumbling in endless cycles. There are huge tree remnants scattered along every beach as far as the eye can see, and roots limbs and trunks all in various stages of decay are proof of violent storms battering away the shoreline. Due to the rotation of the earth, natural prevailing trade winds tend to move from west to east. For example, a flight from California to New York, or across the Atlantic Ocean from America to Europe enjoys a tailwind, while the same returning trip will experience a headwind and take a bit longer. Ocean tides tend to follow similar patterns with currents, and this is why we find most of the West Coast regions to be rough, jagged, and not especially known for warm, inviting beaches. The East Coast, by contrast, has a much gentler coastline, more prone to the occasional tropical depressions, of course, but for the most part this is where you find the best beaches. It's also worth mentioning that all along the eastern shore, you can venture out pretty far in most places before dropping off the continental shelf into deep water, whereas the western side drops off to incredible depths very close to shore, sometimes as little as twenty feet out.

Bridge over Deception Pass in Washington State, a major highway to southern Whidbey Island. On the left side of the bend is exactly where I was standing when two large vehicles collided and I almost got snuffed...
Photo credit to Gary Skiff. (Thank you Gary!)

These are some of the most dangerous waters in the world to navigate, with the tide currents moving around and busting up the coastline, creating hazards for ships large and small.

On your first visit, you might notice some romantic-sounding places like Honeymoon Bay, Lookout Point, and Conception Bluff, but very soon you discover other more ominous-sounding names like Deception Pass, Hurricane Ridge, Go Home Bay, Cape Disappointment, Chilly Bleak, and my all-time favorite, Dismal Nitch.

Sunny days provide a panoramic paradise for photographers with breathtaking vistas in every direction, constantly changing with the angle of the sun, moving cloud formations, and a virtual kaleidoscope of reflecting water. You're hard-pressed to find a bad angle. Very soon you also begin to realize the driving force behind all this, especially as you travel farther north and find more evidence of what shapes the amazingly diverse nature of this region. It's a rain forest, actually, something that normally conjures up images of familiar and more traditional South American jungles, lush, wet, and tropical forests, but here we discover how far north rain forest ecosystems can actually reach.

The greater Seattle Washington region is generally known as a wet-rainy place, and this soggy weather pattern continues north as you pass through Vancouver and into Southeast Alaska. They have very little snow in the coastal regions and there's a reason for that. London, England, for example, is also known for wet, dreary, and fogged-in winter seasons, and for similar reasons.

Latitude-wise they are both well far enough north to experience good amounts of snowfall, but prevailing warm ocean currents push back on the frigid temperatures so that precipitation ends up mostly in the form of rain. The Northwest Pacific region enjoys a warmer Japanese current, similar to the way that some of the Northern Atlantic currents, with help from the prevailing South American currents, affect the overall weather patterns around the United Kingdom.

Several years ago I was invited to be one of three "celebrity" judges for a carving competition in Ocean Shores (Washington State), and an old carving friend met me at Portland airport to continue my journey. Susan lived on a mountain top in northern Oregon, around halfway between the coast and the Cascade Mountains, and from there they could actually watch the infamous Mount St. Helens eruption. In case you're not familiar, St. Helens erupted in 1980, devastating the surrounding area, leveling millions of trees, and sending a huge plume of ash halfway across the country. Susan and Leo also experienced some of the aftermath effects firsthand when the prevailing easterly wind currents reversed on the second day, covering their farm in a thick layer of volcanic ash, which they described as gritty, tiny glass particles with an oily touch that took forever (literally years) to clear away.

I had always had great interest in this grand natural disaster and begged them for a closer look, so we planned a big hike up to the rim for the following day. First we had to swing by their bank for something, and Leo casually mentioned with great surprise that his very first social security retirement check had unexpectedly been processed.

As we got closer to the mountain, it became apparent that everything was still pretty socked in with snow (despite it being June), and a hike to the rim was out of the question, but we were still able to visit the overlook museum, which was very interesting.

I was still hoping to get closer, and as luck would have it we found a little blue tour guide helicopter just set up a few miles down the road. I immediately perked up. We had a quick conference, Leo was all in but Susan was a no-go, she didn't want any part of any little blue "death trap" and didn't try to hide it. She tried pretty hard to talk us out of going by pointing out with great concern that the pilot looked like he was still in high school. (She actually wasn't too far off on that point.) Then she mentioned to Leo, "So this is how you want to spend your first retirement check?"

Finally, she just shrugged her shoulders in resignation and asked Leo for the car keys before we left. "What, in case we don't make it back?" we joked.

A funny side note to the story: I'd been on several different helicopters in the past and for the most part felt pretty comfortable, but this guy was definitely not one with the machine, and eventually confessed that it was the second day of his first week on the job after getting certified, and it hadn't been very busy the previous day. After a quick preflight check, he grabbed the starter switch, first looking around for effect, and proudly announced, "Here we go!" *Click* – and nothing happened. "Oops," he said, "let's try that again." We said, "OK, but that's it, only one oops per trip, right?"

Slightly embarrassed he replied, "OK, here, hold my beer – ha ha, it's an old pilot joke," but he was certainly not an old pilot. He finally got it started and off we went, waving goodbye to poor Susan.

The flight turned out better than expected; the short fifteen-minute trip to the rim and back directly followed the massive mudflow that had completely decimated the enormous valley below, and almost thirty years later it was still a big mess. New growth trees and foliage along with birds and other wildlife were clearly visible from our close overhead proximity, but still in a very much infant stage of recovery compared with the surrounding area. Remnants of large areas of trees bent over to the ground from the initial blast were still visible. It must have felt like an atomic bomb going off, considering the amount of destruction, over such a vast area.

The following day we relaxed before traveling north to the great Olympic Peninsula in Washington, a place I'd always dreamed about seeing and home to no less than seven world record biggest trees, all in close enough proximity to see in one day. (They were western red cedar, Sitka spruce, Douglas fir, yellow cedar, western hemlock, mountain hemlock, and Engelmann spruce.) It was a big day for sure, and a bit of advice if you ever have a chance to do something similar: don't forget your extra camera battery back in the hotel room like some idiots have been known to do…

You'll still come away with great memories, of course, but also miss a once in a lifetime chance to take photos of you and your friends posing alongside big, famous old trees while sharing the history along with interesting facts in this most lovely and photogenic place.

There was so much to see and we tried to fit in as much as possible, but the days flew by and it was time to get back to our original mission: the carving competition in Ocean Shores. To be perfectly honest, I wasn't quite sure what to expect, but Mike and Susan already had a much better idea and actually knew all the competitors. They also explained the awkward side that came along with judging small competitions; somebody was going to win, somebody wasn't, and not to be surprised if there were some hard feelings at the end. To make things even worse, or better, I suppose, depending how you look at things, there were some really amazing carvers and they seemed to be firing on all cylinders, so I knew it was going to be a tough decision.

With over forty years' experience each, Mike and Susan were also prolific carvers in their own right, and I couldn't have been luckier in that regard. However, because they already knew everybody there, I knew it would surely fall on me for any potential tie-breaking vote. The theme was Pirates, the designs were exceptional, and the competition was intense. First place, for example, went to a rendition of the lone survivor straddling the bow of a sinking ship, hands folded in prayer in last-minute hopes of salvation after a lifetime of pillage and plunder.

Second place was a stately-looking wolf standing upright, wearing a jacket and tie with a briefcase by his side, the "Pirates of Wall Street." The other finished pieces, even though less complicated, were all interesting and quite unique as well, so it was indeed a tough decision. I did, however, make an important decision right then and there: I wouldn't do that again.

I've never been comfortable comparing myself with others, we each had our own individual styles, imagination, and skill levels that were all so unique, and what's the point anyhow? Well, to answer my own question, there is a certain public draw to competitions in so many other public venues, so it only stands to reason that it would spill over into the carving realm as well. It does take a special kind of person to pit themselves against others, plus I realize that competitions inspire many people to do their best, and quite a number of carving events today gravitate in that direction. I also think it takes a certain type of person to make a good judge.

Some of the factors go beyond simply being qualified and having had a chance to sit on both sides of the room, well, let me just finish by saying I was happy for the opportunity, it was a lot of fun and a good learning experience as well.

After Ocean Shores wrapped up, I took off with Uncle Mike for a few days. He was anxious to show me some of his favorite places along the way, including Hurricane Ridge; part of an enormous natural park area. Located on the very northern tip of the Olympic Peninsula, the actual ridge is known for its incredible views of the entire region, and accessible only by a long-steep switchback road leading up to the lookout station. The switchback road itself was quite an engineering feat; cut into the mountainside in a such a way that on your right side going up was an almost vertical wall of rock. Coming back down, however, it was a sharp, thousand-foot drop-off with no guard rails, but that comes later, of course.

Largest Sitka Spruce tree in the world, located in the
Valley of Rain Forest Giants, Olympic Peninsula,
Washington state. With a diameter of almost eighteen feet,
it's thought to be around one thousand years old.

From the top was one of the most stunning panoramic views I'd ever seen, cascading mountain ridges fanning out in all directions on such a vast scale that it was nearly impossible to capture in a photo. (But we still try, eh?) We did a short hike but once again were held back by lingering snowdrifts blocking the trail, and just as well. Mike was just getting warmed up with a running tutorial about the formation and recent history of the entire region, which included tales of the old timber logging days. He was an encyclopedia of knowledge around this subject and told them in such a way that you could understand he had, at one time or other, some personal firsthand experience. He was also a big guy to begin with and would sometimes hold his arms out in an animated way to illustrate something even bigger, all the while mixing in stories about personal friends and their struggles trying to make a living in such a hostile environment.

The ride back down was memorable as well. Mike was a bit of a weaver behind the wheel, drifting off toward one side and suddenly catching himself, then he would overcompensate a bit and start drifting over to the other side. A moment later he would look off in another direction and start to weave that way, which normally wouldn't be such a big deal, except this time it was a thousand-foot drop, with no guard rails, straight to the bottom. At some point I actually started to get a massive leg cramp from pressing on the floor, trying to slow us down and finally growled at him, "Damn it, Mike, slow down, I'm trying to take some pictures here." To that he would instantly apologize and slow down for a short while, but pretty soon start picking up speed and weaving again.

I don't think he would make a very good helicopter pilot, but other than that he is truly one of the most interesting people I've ever met, and it was a real treat to have someone so knowledgeable like him as a personal guide.

After a couple fun days running around with Mike, I was passed on yet again to another native "left coaster" who was an old friend, Steve Backus, who also happened to be Mike's nephew. Steve was the organizer of the Ocean Shores competition and it amazed me that such a vast region could still feel like a fairly small community. In a land of big and hearty people, Steve still managed to stand out from most others, and in a lot of ways. He too was anxious to show me his favorite places on this next leg of my journey and our first stop was Deception Pass. Discovered by George Vancouver, but later named by the even more famous Captain James Cook while he searched for the fabled Northwest Passage, it was yet another place I had always dreamed about seeing.

It was now a state park and recreational area, and the focal point was a massive high arch-type bridge with amazing views of the surrounding area, and a pedestrian walkway across the entire structure. Below were the boiling waters where private boaters pass through into Skagit Bay, but only when timed according to the tide charts. At times you could see a small flotilla grouping up and waiting for the right moment. This was risky business, however, even for experienced boaters as the currents could either hold you back, or push you along at fifteen knots, where one little mistake could prove disastrous.

I too had a close call; standing on the bridge that particular day, I was moving toward another spot to find a good camera angle, and just where the road bent toward the middle of the bridge is where it happened. A large southbound tractor-trailer truck happened to converge on the exact same spot at the same time as a long motor home coming in the other direction. It was an unexpected tight maneuver for both and the back ends of their vehicles collided. I'm pretty sure they were both going too fast and I truly expected one, or perhaps both, to go over the edge, taking me along with them while spiraling into the abyss. I'm not one to brag or complain much but will make an exception for that particular incident. At this exact moment I thought it was the end, and years later friends would remember me as "a nice guy, but in the wrong place at the right time." Almost within arm's reach, I helplessly watched those two high-speed behemoths start to wobble, and in a fleeting moment realized that I had reached a critical point in my life. Fortunately for all of us, they both recovered at the very last second or otherwise you wouldn't be reading these *Chainsaw Chronicles* right now, eh?

Steve was somewhere else at that moment but afterward he noticed my knees still shaking a bit and asked what had happened. I explained everything, hoping for a spot of sympathy, but he just made a joke about how it was low tide and it would be better swimming if I'd waited awhile. (Never mind the two-hundred-foot drop, right?) Later that day we headed off toward Whidbey Island, hoping to catch the last ferry. I asked Steve if he knew any shortcuts. "Sure, of course I do," he said, "but we don't have enough time for any of that."

If you've ever had a chance to meet or know somebody who is funny all the time, even without trying to be, that is Steve, and it's infectious just to be around him. He's also almost twice my size, but we have a number of things in common, for example, a shared appreciation for the absurd, a passion for reading, and metaphorically speaking a desire to leave campsites a little cleaner than we found them. I have met most of his large and extended family of other carving legends on the West Coast and this story could not be complete without saying a few words about them.

Steve's mother, Judy McVay, for example, has been carving for over fifty years and was the very first female chainsaw carver in America, which probably means the first in the world, as well. Judy is almost single-handedly responsible for chainsaw carving finding its way into the official classification of "folk art," which I explain in greater detail in another chapter. Judy has both children and grandchildren who carve at a professional level and I suspect that before very long it will be great-grandchildren as well. Her two brothers are prolific carvers too; one is Pat, whom I had a chance to meet and spend some time with on a trip to Scotland a few years ago. The other is Uncle Mike, whom I mentioned above.

My favorite part about spending time with Steve is the storytelling, and he has more stories than anybody I have ever met. Some are about their early times of scratching out a living in-and-around the Olympic Peninsula, then later on Whidbey Island, struggling for many years, and how anytime he would ask for money, his mom would growl at him to just get outside and carve some bears.

Plus he is a walking history book of carvers from the Left Coast, many of whom never owned a cell phone, let alone a computer, and other than a few newspaper scrapings their accomplishments would be lost forever. I could fill pages with stories from just the ones I know of, but Steve has so many more and oftentimes he can fill in the cracks on a personal level, telling tales of debauchery from the night before and many of them are best left for intimate campfire time.

Another Left Coaster story revolves around a mutual friend and carver who I was introduced to through the US mail a number of years ago. The National Woodcarvers Association publishes a bimonthly magazine called *Chip Chats*, of which I have been a contributing columnist for almost twenty years. My little spot covers chainsaw carving, and through this I've come to know a good number of carvers from all across the country, becoming friends with many of them. It's been great fun sharing stories and some candid advice, plus an early outlet for writing, of which I always have always enjoyed.

Keep in mind, this publication and my little spot began way before the Internet, so letters had to be answered by hand, if you can still remember those days? One particular guy was writing from a prison in Washington State. He was pretty young and an aspiring carver before things went south in his life. Eventually he shared the details around that and it really was quite unfortunate, so over the next few years we communicated fairly often. I would send him particular carving information, some chisels, even a knife, and I was always surprised they allowed it.

One day he very excitedly wrote to say that the guards got him a chainsaw, under certain restrictions of course, but chainsaw carving in prison? I'm pretty sure that was a first. Written words are truly a window into the soul and from getting to know him through our letters, I had a sense that he was a good person who got caught up in some bad luck, but overall he was a really nice guy. This was confirmed by the friendships he made with the guards who allowed him to use a chainsaw inside a state penitentiary.

At some point we lost touch and it was quite a few years before our paths crossed again and we finally had a chance to meet in person. It was during this trip that I happened to mention his name and my friends said: "Oh yes, we know him. Matter of fact, he has a business not far from here if you want to surprise him sometime?"

A day or two later we drove along the Oregon coast and found his quaint little oceanfront tourist town, and then his shop. It was such fun; he was carving away on something, glanced over at us and went back to work. Then a couple minutes later he looked over again and recognized my friend Susan, and a moment later his eyes focused on me and he suddenly realized who I was. He dropped the saw, came running over and lifted me off the ground in a big bear hug. Grinning from ear to ear, he said, "Joe King!"

What great fun it was to finally meet him, and even more so to discover how well he was doing with his carving business. He was also happily married (or soon to be) and starting a family. We talked for a little while but soon had to move on up the coast toward our next destination, and I marveled at another one of life's little circles coming to fruition.

Mike McVay- my friend and travel guide with his on-going tutorial about the regional demographic history of the Pacific Northwest.

Nine

Culture Shock #7

Culture shock comes in many forms, quite often unexpected, and in my humble opinion it happens more so the farther east you travel around the world. This particular situation happened at Kazansky train station in Moscow, just prior to our scheduled overnight ride to Cheboksary. Domestic flights are more common now, but trains had been the lifeline of the country for over a century and many of their stations were like old-world museums. Big, beautiful ornate buildings with marble floors, colorful ceramic mosaic designs covering walls and ceilings alike, and the most disgusting restrooms on the planet. (Although I've never been to China.) In Kazansky, there were also some nice little kiosk-type cafés in the main hallway. They were tempting, but I had more urgent business and hurried along to find the closest toilet. At this time you still had to pay, but I expected that and was prepared with some small change and almost threw it at the cashier lady who then tried to ask me something I didn't quite understand. It was a most critical time, so I hurried on through, pretending not to hear her, which was turned out to be a big mistake. It was a fairly large room, that was also probably quite eloquent in its day, but not anymore. Off to one side was the normal row of dirty old sinks with some guys shaving and having a quick sponge bath. On the other side was my destination: a long line of Asian-style toilets, which were little more than a hole in the floor with little cement "put feet here" imprints.

Most of them had flimsy wooden privacy dividers, but they were all occupied except for one on the closest side, almost in the middle of the room. Just a hole with no wall, but I was running out of time and pretty much desperate at this point, so every last crumb of dignity went straight out the window and I had at it.

If you've ever been lucky enough to experience this type of facility, you may recall what a balancing act it can be; coordination is essential. Speaking from personal experience, and sorry in advance for being so graphic, it's not just about just trying to center over a little hole in a full squat position, but holding your jeans up off of the nasty floor with one hand while trying really hard not to drop something important from your other pockets, like a cell phone or tickets. I imagine it gets easier with practice, but I was in a bit of a spot, and just as I just got settled in, it suddenly occurred me what the cashier lady was asking: "Do you want paper too?"

Yikes…

On the way in I had noticed the ever-present little old cleaning lady. (I really shouldn't say "old lady" because with a big, heavy overcoat and traditional scarf covering her head, you couldn't guess her age even if you tried.) In a moment of brilliant desperation I found money in my jacket, held it up in the air and called out, "*Babushka, pozhaluysta*," (Grandma, please). Luckily for me, she actually was a little old lady, very kind, and in hindsight I'm also pretty sure I wasn't the first person who ever found themselves in that situation. She shuffled right over and was well prepared with a pocket full of paper. She counted out seven little sheets and went about her business.

It was an American twenty-dollar bill I handed over, possibly half a week's pay for her and roughly three dollars a sheet for me, a wee bit high but it was no time for negotiations; sometimes salvation comes at a hefty price.

Trying hard to always keep an open mind, culture shock continued throughout my first few trips to Russia, to the point where I began numbering them. Number eleven was during a taxi ride to the airport with Nelli, where I made a serious faux pas. (My dad used to make jokes about "fox paws" all the time). There was an old Rod Stewart love song playing on the radio, I was leaving and she was staying, both lost in a bittersweet moment and I started to softly whistle along with the song when our driver immediately growled at Nelli, "Tell him stop whistling inside the car, it's bad luck and maybe I'll get no money this day."

By this time I was already catching on to some of the old customs; for example, you must never shake hands or hug in a doorway, it's necessary to step out or come completely inside first. I was also cautioned not to whistle in public, as people would think I was drunk, or gay, or even worse – both! But I did sometimes anyhow. There are so many marble and cement buildings, including passageways under busy intersections, and sometimes it's too hard to resist. It feels like suddenly walking into an acoustic sound chamber, so I would break out in a loud whistle and embarrass my friends. (Yes, I am a whistler.) So by then I should have already guessed that it wasn't okay to do so in a car, and the driver got really upset. Nelli was slightly bothered as well (at the driver) and tried to smooth it over by explaining that I was an American, everybody whistles there and they have lots of money.

"Well, that might be true," he growled back, "but tell him it's my taxi and if he does it again, I'm throwing his American ass out."

So of course I immediately stopped, and unfortunately it turned out to be a self-fulfilling prophecy for this poor guy. I normally leave a tip but didn't this time thinking, *Too bad for you, fellow, you could have bought some new wiper blades or something.* (It was *screech, scratch, screech, scratch* all the way to the airport.) We arrived exactly on time and afterward I regretted not leaving a tip, as many of us get stuck on old habits in one form or other, but more importantly I missed a great opportunity to soften another American stereotype.

I love going into little stores wherever we travel. It can be like a slice of local culture, but be prepared for some less-than-friendly service in some of the smaller ones. There are two questions you'll be asked every time when checking out: "Do you want a bag?" (*Da* or *nyet*.) And, "Don't you have smaller change?" The latter is more important as you can and will actually be turned away on occasion if the answer is *nyet*. They also have persistent security guards who take great pleasure in following anybody around who looks different, or unusual, like me, for example. On one particular occasion I was looking through a big display of bar-type bath soap. It was really well made with different organic and slightly fruit-scented options, real quality, in my opinion. That time, however, a young store employee was following us and watching my every move. Around every corner there she was, so I finally had to ask, "What the heck are you watching me for? I'm visiting from America and do you really think I'm going to risk getting arrested for stealing a bar of soap?"

She smiled slightly and in a somewhat embarrassed way explained, "Sorry, it's my job."

I suddenly thought back to the taxi incident and became a little embarrassed myself as well. It's not possible to fully immerse yourself into another culture without being completely open to every little experience that comes along, like it or not. But this is how we learn.

Wood carvers especially enjoy learning about different countries with their own version of mythical or folklore figures from the unforgotten past: trolls, gnomes, elves, ogres, and a myriad of other imaginary characters. In Russia it's *Domovoi*, "He of the house."

Normally it goes by a cat during the day and roams freely around the village, but transforms each night into a kindly-looking and sometimes ragged-type character who wanders around helping those in need. This can include, but is not limited to, little personal favors like mending clothes, combing your hair while you're asleep, fixing a broken chair, weeding the garden, or even looking through a new apartment ahead of time to chase away any bad spirits that might be hanging around. Domovoi is well represented in the carving and statue realm as well, and I have a nice one too, gifted from a friend. He's holding a fluffy cat in his arms with a far-off look as though searching for his next good deed, and very much resembles a close relative of Saint Nicholas. His name actually comes up quite often in our house, like when something goes missing, or is unexpectedly found, we simply blame or credit this to Domovoi.

I've had a chance to celebrate my birthday in some other countries over the years, seven times to be exact, and although I always try to hide it from my friends, they always find out. Each time, however, it has turned out to be an absolutely memorable experience, including two times in Russia, which stand out.

During summer it's old Russian tradition to have the party in a forest (if it coincides, of course), and by coincidence our friend Olga's birthday coincided with mine, plus another close friend just days before. How lucky was that? It was an absolutely beautiful late August afternoon with just a slight hint of autumn in the air, but everything was still in full bloom, and especially the wonderful birch leaves, which were just starting to turn yellow against their white trunk and limbs.

As usual, there was an amazing amount of food, many different types of fresh salad, which were mostly picked that very morning, plus various potato, beet, and tomato dishes prepared ahead of time, and the main entrée: kebabs over a campfire. Off to one side of the fire pit and half buried in the embers, I noticed a pot of fish soup simmering away with ingredients including, but not limited to, carrots, onions, garlic, potatoes, one large whole fish, plus some other unidentifiable items. Toward the end, someone threw in a chunk of burning ember from the fire and nobody seemed to notice but me, so I had to ask, "What's up with that?" No less than six different answers followed ranging from seasoning, honoring old spirits, good luck, and some others that didn't translate so well. For some strange reason it made me think of Domovoi.

The afternoon progressed into some silly party games mixed in with more drinking. For example, all the girls all lined up and it began with, "Who is oldest one here?" All stepped back except for one, next it was who had the smallest shoe size, and again all stepped back except the winner, and so it went with a barrage of other challenges like tallest, biggest chest, and so on.

Nothing was sacred, and everybody already knew everybody, so there was absolutely no possible way to cheat. It was all great fun to watch until the next game where the men were all shuffled into a little group and it was our turn. The idea was to physically represent some natural form aligned with the season in which you were born, a bit like the American version of charades. The main difference, however, was that we were in a forest surrounded by a group of mostly drunk Russians.

Surprisingly it didn't feel that much different to other forest parties I had been to in the past. After all, people are people and forests are forests. More funny games followed, but I'm sorry to report that I cannot remember much after that except toward the end as final toasts were being made. Olga went first, the birthday girl, getting all serious and you could hear a pin drop in the forest as she pulled us all in close (and a bit teary-eyed, I noticed), then in broken English made her most sincere toast: "Joseph, Nelli, you love you – let's have baby! I am Olga!"

Every country has its particular traditional spirits: Mexico has tequila, Scotland with its Scotch, schnapps in Germany, bourbon in the States, and in Russia, of course, its vodka. This is an unavoidable experience if you spend any amount of time there, but for the most part it felt more like mixing fun and tradition as opposed to all-out drunken debauchery as portrayed in many stereotypical images. Food was shared around tables and piled high with everything you can think of, and the entire evening was spent sitting around the table where we ate, toasted, and repeated.

I should also explain the rules: There was no such thing as sipping in Russia, absolutely no mixing of the vodka with orange juice or a splash of cranberry juice, it was always a straight bottoms up by the shot glass. By the end of the night a fair amount has been consumed, but mixed with such an abundance of food that it was not such an inebriated experience as you might imagine. Nobody was falling down drunk, except for me one time when I fell down the steps in my own house, but that's another story.

By the end of the night there was always a big pot of chai (black tea) brewing, that everyone shared before heading off for home.

On the subject of drinking habits, there is an old story about Peter the Great having a childhood friend who turned out to be the town drunk. It was obviously an embarrassing situation for the Czar, but he still had a soft spot in his heart for his old buddy who was constantly trying to find a way in and ask for money. As the story goes, just to rid himself of the nuisance, he had his official mark tattooed on the guy's neck so that from that point on all he had to do was walk into any pub, pull his collar down, flick his neck a couple times and drink for free all night long.

Regardless of whether or not the story is true, until this very day when your Russian friend or acquaintance pulls their collar down and 'flicks the neck,' it's a universal signal to break out the vodka. You can actually test this for yourself sometime if you happen to have a Russian friend. Tilt your head back slightly when you do it and just watch their reaction, which will range from surprise that you know about this old custom, or "Okay, sure, let's do it."

The Russian word for beer is *piva* (peeva), and a can of beer, for example, would be *bunka piva*. But keep in mind this is a gender-based language so the can is a *he*, and the beer is a *she*, understand, right? Beer was not overly popular there, but I sense that changing, and recently found some on tap in the local Burger King. Three brands!

Most of the American fast-food chains like McDonald's, KFC, Pizza Hut, and some others are very popular there now and don't be surprised: they're just as bad as in the US. (Except they all sell beer) Of course you need to try one sometime in order to complete your travel research, otherwise it's a complete waste of time, given all the great traditional restaurants you can find on almost every corner. A warm bowl of borscht—traditional beet and cabbage soup with a dollop of sour cream on top—or a thick slice of bacon fat on the side is extremely popular. But not for me, I go straight for meat pierogi's or fish pie. Dairy products are also a treat; rich and flavorful, and everything is graded by a number right on the package. Because of that, their chocolate tends to be super rich and tasty as well. I have been known to fill a carry-on backpack completely to the top and will say more about that in a later chapter.

I could actually fill pages talking about Russian cuisine; it is really quite amazing, but let me just summarize with this one little fact: Russia has the best candy and ice cream in the world.

Ten

Loosiana ...

In August of 2005, the massive Hurricane Katrina devastated New Orleans, along with much of the adjoining region, and some months later I had a chance to travel there with a handful of other carvers to do volunteer work and fundraising events. Small pockets of the city were somewhat untouched, but surrounded by areas of total devastation on such a massive scale it's hard to describe.

We were invited by a local organizer who arranged some different opportunities to help, and the first venue was a three-day music and seafood festival in Plaquemines Parish. What I didn't know at the time was that a "parish" in Louisiana is another word for county, so I thought, "Oh great, a bunch of nuns, we'll to have to hide the beer." My fears were short-lived, however. While setting up on the first morning, we noticed several large beer trucks rolling in and straight away they opened up for business. Next came a small parade of other festival vendors, including various Cajun seafood booths, plus a stage with ongoing authentic music from the "Loosiana Bayou." It felt like a spot of normalcy in a sea of total chaos that stretched for miles in every direction, and we seemed to fit right in. There were four of us carvers, one girl from Canada, a couple guys from Wisconsin and Louisiana, and me. It was midsummer and extremely hot, so we immediately pulled our tents together in a square to make some shade (a precious commodity) before getting down to business.

A little later in the morning we heard the steady *chomp, chomp, chomp* of something getting closer, and all of a sudden the cutest little red helicopter came over the horizon and settled in right close to us. It was from a local tour guide company and I thought, *Wow, this is getting better by the minute.* We had beer on the left, food on the right, live music right up front, and now a helicopter had joined in. It wasn't a very busy morning yet for anyone, except the beer trucks of course, so by lunchtime we had already made friends with the pilot who seemed to be interested in us as well. We also had the only shade around and a little bit of that goes a long way on scorching hot summer days like that one. The pilot loved the carvings and mentioned how much his mom had always wanted one, so I said, "OK, go ahead pick one out, it's on the house."

He couldn't decide which one at first but had it narrowed down to two, so I insisted that he go ahead and take them both, and it worked; we now had our own private helicopter anytime we wanted for the next three days, and I ask you, how cool is that? The pilot was a super nice guy and being from the area, he knew exactly the most interesting places to see, plus you could say things like, "Oh look, what's down there?" And a moment later he would break into a turning drop and spiral right in like a news channel's "eye in the sky."

A surprising amount of people turned out and the four of us were kept quite busy carving throughout the weekend, so by the end we managed to raise a good amount of money for the cause. Plus we ate well, met some interesting people along the way, and best of all, a had bird's-eye view of New Orleans like few others have ever had a chance to enjoy.

Our personal helicopter while carving at the seafood festival in Plaquemines Parish. Below: the simple controls. Looks easy, right?

But I'm getting ahead of myself. A local sheriff pulled in on the second morning with a van loaded up with a genuine and real life "Loosiana chain gang," just like in a movie. The guys spilled out of their vehicle and immediately headed straight for the closest shade they could find, which of course was us. Other than being convicts, they turned out to be a really nice and friendly bunch of guys and we had a lot of fun together talking, laughing and posing for photos. We were basically just a bunch of carvers and criminals hanging out together.

The sheriff was an interesting guy and looked like he could be straight out of a movie as well; he was very calm and laid back, but you could tell by how the others behaved around him that he was probably the last guy in the world to mess with. All in all it turned out to be a fun morning, but eventually we all needed to get back to work and unanimously decided not to trade a carving to go for a ride in the prisoner's van.

The third morning was interesting as well when a local Boy Scouts troop pulled in and set up for the day right near us, and it was a similar scenario; they set up their little camp and headed straight for the nearest shade. The kids were over-the-top excited to find a group of carvers and being a former troop leader myself, it was most enjoyable.

One of their troop leaders and I got friendly and he mentioned that he was a navy officer, second in command at the nearby joint naval / air force base. I had seen photos of the place on the news reports as it was ground zero for the massive emergency rescue effort, and he offered to show me around the base.

After attending to a few details, we both slipped away and what followed was a grand tour of all their ships, helicopters, and a number of other military-type vehicles.

In the first hanger we walked into, he introduced me as, "A famous chainsaw artist from Pennsylvania, who has come all the way down here to help. Let's show him around, boys." Those guys were great too. They dropped what they were doing and took turns sharing personal stories about what it was actually like during the worst part of the rescue operation. Some of them were already in the air before the hurricane had passed and pulling people off of rooftops in sixty-mile-an-hour winds, then piling them in, ten or fifteen at a time, in a helicopter designed to hold no more than eight. There were many close calls as they worked around the clock with short naps in-between, and most of them had no contact with their own families at home right from the beginning.

Up until that point in time almost everybody we had met was courteous and friendly, and genuinely appreciative of us volunteering to help in our own little way. We were equally humbled by how well they treated us, and despite the oppressive heat, we were also having the time of our lives.

Toward the end of the festival, our organizer said that their local state representative had heard about our little project and wanted to meet us. It was good PR so we cleaned up a bit and drove off to find his office. One of the carvers with us was Burt Fleming who lived fairly close by and was somewhat familiar with New Orleans. He happened to mention on the way over that he wasn't very fond of politicians and didn't mind saying so, and we were all having some fun with that.

The representative turned out to be a super nice guy, however, very personable and genuine in thanking us for coming down to volunteer. We had a nice long photo session in the blessed air conditioning, so nobody was in a hurry to leave.

I started poking at Burt to get in on it too because we all knew how un-fond he was of politicians, and this might have been his best and last chance to "cross the aisle." He just rolled his eyes and moseyed on over, grabbed the guy in a big man hug and growled at him, "Okay, smile and pretend like we like each other." They made eye contact for a moment and both broke out in spontaneous laughter just as I snapped the camera, and it turned out to be a great photo. Burt's wife had it put on their coffee mugs not long after that when this same guy got elected as Louisiana's fifty-fifth state governor (Bobby Jindal).

"Loosiana" is of course local slang, and like many of the other deep Southern states, they move at a slightly different pace compared to other parts of the country, but understandably so, due to the hot, humid conditions. It's not quite siesta climate, but very close, and this also reflects in their slow, drawn-out accents, which "we of the north" made endless jokes about. But it's not entirely unfounded; nobody's wasted any extra syllables in order to pronounce something the way we expect to hear it, in fact some of the accents were so strong I almost needed a translator. And like other strong accents around the world, forget about ever having a reasonable phone conversation.

I should also mention before moving on to the next part, in no way do I mean to make light of such a terrible situation.

We personally met many people who experienced great loss and all of us left there wishing that we could do more.

Unfortunately, that wasn't my first natural disaster experience. The first time was in my early twenties when the second-most famous Johnstown flood happened in 1977. And yes, there were two, in case you're not familiar.

As terrible as it was, it paled in comparison to the Great Flood of 1989, which was actually the third worst in US history in terms of human loss. My father was sent there immediately by the utility company he worked for. It was an emergency situation and he pretty much lived there for the next few months. On Saturday nights he would return home for a short visit then head back out the following afternoon, and on one such visit he encouraged me to go and do some volunteer work to see what it was really like.

The following week I convinced a couple of friends to come along and off we went with truly no idea what to expect. Johnstown was built in one of the big Western Pennsylvania mountain valleys, and driving down into it that morning felt like descending into hell. National Guard troops had the entire area cordoned off while emergency crews combed back and forth through the devastation, which at this point had changed from a rescue to recovery operation. Dad had given me an "all-access" essential worker tag for my truck, otherwise we would never have been permitted to enter the valley.

Toward the end of the day, I found Dad and he introduced us to a guy he made friends with who was kind of a town drunk-type character, and he agreed to be our personal tour guide for a six-pack of beer. I certainly don't mean to make light of such a terrible situation and only mention this part as it allowed us to see things even the media wasn't privy to. The typical work crews operated in three-man teams: a dump truck driver, a high lift operator loading the dump truck, and a third guy sitting on top of the dump truck cab watching every scoop going in for bodies as they were still finding a good many.

(Earlier in the day, a body was found in the mud-filled basement of a church where my friends and I were working.) As in the earlier flood, the devastation was spread along a wide path up through the valleys toward its source, and pockets of bizarre devastation were scattered around, seemingly at random. An overall dank smell lingered everywhere and that was one of the parts that gave everything such a surreal feeling that was burned into memory.

Looking back on this experience, I have come to realize what a profound effect it had on my thinking and reactions around crisis, loss and personal devastation, and how people deal with it. New Orleans would be many years in the future, but the firsthand experience of a natural disaster like that is something that has stayed with me forever. (Including the value of a good local guide. Thanks, Dad!)

Not long after returning from that great adventure, I lost my house as well; it was totally destroyed by fire and nothing could have prepared me for that.

This was an old condemned property, and I was in the final stages of remodeling and preparing to sell it soon, in order to afford a nicer place. I was actually just returning home and the street was blocked off with fire trucks with smoke everywhere, and I suddenly realized that it was my house burning.

The next part was kind of a blur, like in a half-awake bad dream and I can only remember bits and pieces. I knew that my wife and small son were home at this time and started running towards the fire when a neighbor tackled me in the street and said, "It's OK, they're safe and in our house."

The next person who stopped me was Woody DelBane, who was my parents' neighbor, and also the firemen's chief. He asked me, "Who's house is this, Joey?" I stood there watching them try to extinguish the flames for a while, and remember it being the most empty feeling I had ever experienced. On one hand, my family were safe and that was a source of overwhelming relief, but on the other hand, I was witnessing firsthand everything I owned go up in flames. Later that night we had to stop and buy some little things like a toothbrush and other personal items as there was absolutely nothing left from where we had started out that very morning.

It wasn't until many years later that I realized how a sudden traumatic situation can so fundamentally change people, and began to understand what they now define as PTSD (post-traumatic stress disorder). At the time I was already a collector of sorts, old guitars, custom knives, an antique tool collection, things like that, which were much easier to find back then.

Picking through the rubble I would come across burnt, melted remnants that seemed so important at the time, but were now all headed for a garbage dumpster.

I came away from the experience with a newfound appreciation for life, but more importantly, the realization of how fragile it really is. Plus I developed somewhat of a disregard for material items. This is actually a problem sometimes as I am now the biggest un-collector you're likely to meet, or a "minimalist" as they say. Yes, I still enjoy and appreciate nice things and keep a few precious collectables around, but somewhere in the back of my subconscious lingers a realization that everything we hold dear can be taken away in one unexpected moment. A traumatic experience either beats us down or makes us stronger, or perhaps a little of both. So wake up tomorrow and thank God for one more day.

My friend Burt Fleming (right) with Bobby Jindal who would later go on to become the governor of Louisiana.

Eleven

Rendezvous ...

It was a cold, blustery night as we came up over the ridge above Ridgway. The road finally opened up into extra lanes and it. was a big relief as the weather was starting to get nasty. Suddenly I noticed red lights flashing behind us and thought, *What's the emergency?* But there wasn't an emergency, it was actually a police car following me going for going too fast. Unfortunately not the first time it had ever happened, but the most embarrassing for sure.

I had a big custom-size personal van at the time with a lot of seats, and we had just collected a French carving family from the Pittsburgh airport. Everyone was in the back except for Paquet, who was sitting beside me in the passenger's seat and looking through my photo album. He didn't speak very much English but knew exactly what was happening and found the words: "Happens all the time for me." His wife and two sons were in the back seats and one of them had his camera ready and snapped a flash photo at the trooper just as he got to the window to ask for my information. Suddenly, it was a tense moment. After regaining his composure from the sudden flash, he looked through the window and asked Piquet something, to which he just shrugged and mumbled something in French. By this point the trooper started getting suspicious, so I began to ramble on about how we had just picked them up at the airport.

"Which airport?" he interrupted. I told him, and mentioned that we had been driving for almost four hours through this crappy weather, and we're late for the Rendezvous. "Oh, the Rendezvous," he said. "You one of them carvers?" "Yes, of course," I explained, and as luck would have it, my photo book was still sitting on the console, so I just handed it over, instead of the owners card he was asking for. He immediately perked up and began looking through some pictures, asking questions about certain ones, then finally said, "Well, OK, you slow down and when you see one of the Boni Brothers, tell them I still have those pine logs. They're behind the barn; just come over anytime."

Glancing over my shoulder, even in the darkness, I could see the boys bubbling over in excitement to see their first American policeman. Paquet's wife was in total mortification, and my girlfriend, who was sitting beside her, had a finger in her own mouth, pantomiming forced vomit and disbelief like, *is this really happening*?

No chainsaw chronicle would be complete without tales of the great Rendezvous. Modern artist communities can go international almost overnight these days with help from the Internet, but this helpful tool was just beginning around twenty years ago when my friends started the "Ridgway Chainsaw Carving Rendezvous" in the remote little north central Pennsylvania town of Ridgway. The first year only a handful of carving buddies got together. There weren't very many of us back then, or so we thought, but before long they were coming out of the woodwork, so to speak.

The following year it went up to twenty-two and eventually started growing well into the hundreds in a very short few years, each time establishing new records for this type of event. Almost from the beginning, carvers from many other countries began discovering "the Vous," as it became known, telling others about it, and most of them returning year after year.

This truly was *the* place to be for beginners, plus old hands, and anybody else who had interest in carving was drawn to this new carving Mecca. A few were local, but most others came from all across the country and quite literally all corners of the world. On the surface it was a motley-looking crew and almost immediately took on kind of a tribal feel.

Chainsaw carving was barely on the map at this point in time and the concept of a gathering like this was really something new. Some would say it was even magical. Most of the people would bring their families along as well, whenever possible, and this unexpected twist actually took the whole experience to the next level as we all started to mix and develop friendships.

During the day us carvers would be out there carving our hearts away, sharing ideas, techniques, and connecting on a level we could never have imagined before. At the same time our families were pretty much doing the same thing: making new friends, sharing experiences and overall just enjoying this newfound camaraderie.

Most of us would also gather in the evenings for large group dinners, then afterward head over to the local café or pubs.

Any place with a stage for music or open mic nights was much preferred as many of us were musicians as well, and this always added fuel to the fun, which oftentimes went on well into the night. And yes, even got a bit rowdy at times.

I remember reading about the famous French Renaissance with artists collaborating with one another, some competing for recognition, but most of them simply following a passion to push the boundaries of their own individual talents and taking full advantage of the shared learning experience. And it was the same with us; some of the similarities are striking if you look closer. Families were mixing and forming lifetime bonds, and there were some milestones as well: a few marriages, at least three conceptions that we know of for sure, and of course a few scandals. That was to be expected; however, such a big collection of free spirits and mixed cultures always made for an interesting experience. The sheer diversity also evolved over the years and I remember one time we had almost twenty Japanese and thirty-one female carvers in attendance, which certainly must have been some kind of new world record.

The town of Ridgway is around a four-hour drive from the Pittsburgh airport and sometimes there were flight delays to contend with as well. I was living (part-time) in Pittsburgh at the time, so being the closest one it was often my job to collect the overseas families. Most of the international flights would arrive later in the evening, making it unpractical for the long drive to Ridgway, so we would end up keeping them overnight, which almost always made for an interesting experience.

Early on we began to realize that some of them had never been out of their own country before and were a bit nervous to venture "off the island," as the Brits would say. But they all had some things in common like tired and hungry, a bit nervous, but most of all very excited to get to the Rendezvous.

One of many classic examples from the early days went as follows: Some of the families were traveling from the United Kingdom where "mad cow disease" was in full swing, and we knew about that, so the first thing we would do is warm up the grill, throw those guys in the Jacuzzi with a cold beer, then cook up some fat, juicy steaks.

It was funny to watch them eat, as at first they would go really slow which confused us, and we wondered if maybe they didn't like it. The next thing we knew, the steak was completely gone and they were chewing on the bone, savoring every morsel and also looking completely relaxed by this time. Stepping off a plane into a foreign country and being met by a complete stranger takes a bit of nerve, especially if it's your first time. This is something I have also experienced. When the stranger turns out to be a kind person who takes you right in and immediately makes you feel right at home is how we sometimes make a friend for life.

We also started to realize at this time how corrupt and slanted our news agencies can be, and on both sides. For example; One year the Gulf war of 1991 had just started and most of our European friends nearly cancelled thinking that all America was a giant war machine, when in fact most of us didn't want to have any part of that.

A typical airport run; including carvers from Scotland,
Sweden, Finland, and me in the middle, next to Angie

What happened next was even better. Almost
from the beginning we were able to attract some extra
attention in areas such as sponsorship and media exposure
because it was an international event happening right there
in our own little backyard. Afterward, the visiting
international carvers would return home with new ideas
and inspiration to start similar carving events in their own
country, so before long some of us were getting invitations
from all over the world, and this was truly the beginning of
my own personal international travels. It really was quite a
wonderful way to see a new country for the first time, as I
described above, when friends collect you from the
airport, settle you in, and then show you around their
personal favorite local places. That is the true magic of
travel for me and can you imagine that oftentimes it can be
all-expenses-paid?

Even better than that, as many times I would return home with more money than I started out with!

The first overseas carving adventure I attended was sponsored by the Living Heritage Country Festivals promoters in England, and held at Sandringham, the Queen's summer estate. Our friend Dennis Heath was instrumental in organizing the carving side. He had already been demonstrating for them over the years and proposed the idea.

Dennis also had an interesting experience the first time he participated. Part way through the second day a man in a black suit came over to his spot, interrupted him and said, "The Queen would like to meet you." Minutes later a number of other "suits" (as he called them) surrounded his area and there she was – Queen Elizabeth. Dennis is not physically a big man, fairly close in size to her, actually, and I have a photo from the moment they first met. They were shaking hands and she simply said, "Lovely, lovely." Try as hard as he could, Dennis explained, he couldn't force out a single word. "I was quite gob-smacked," he later recounted.

That time in Sandringham there were fifty-seven carvers representing the twelve different countries in attendance, and one of the highlights was the daily speed carve. Everyone who chose to participate had exactly thirty minutes to produce something, then immediately afterward an auctioneer would take over and the proceeds went directly to us for some extra pocket money. It was very exciting; they had a fenced-in area about half the size of a football field lined with crowds of four-to-five-people deep, surrounding and cheering us on.

They also used a state-of-the-art speaker system with music blasting away while a commentator kept up a running dialogue:

"Hello, everyone, and welcome to the second annual English Open Chainsaw Carving Competition. Carvers from around the world have come together to demonstrate their talent, and wait a minute, here's one now, it's Joe King from America. Tell us, Joe, how is it today?"

It was great fun spending time with all of the international carvers, many of whom had brought their families along with them. It was all so very exciting and went by so fast. All too soon it was over, and a handful of us were shuttled up north to the "wee shire" of Carrbridge, Scotland, for a one-day festival, plus several additional days of fun and exploration.

I have some close friends who lived not far from there and were anxious to show me some of their favorite spots as well, including Inverness, home of Nessie, the well-known Loch Ness Monster. (The cover photo of this book was taken not far from there.) This was the first of three visits to the Highlands and as usual we were all invited to the annual Cèilidh, a most festive traditional Scottish party with many locals attending, that always lasted well into the night. The pronunciation is something like "kay-lee" and included dancing to Gaelic folk music, and some drinking of the Scotch.

Another great experience was the first time having a chance to hear a pipe band perform; a group of bagpipe players of all size and ages, and in my opinion there is no other sound in the world that can send a shiver through your body like live bagpipes.

One other quick personal note here if you don't mind: I think Scottish women have absolutely the sweetest accent in all of the world.

The 'Highland Cattle' were everywhere, but not nearly as many as sheep who greatly outnumber people.

Chainsaw carving pretty much started in America, or perhaps I should say we are to blame for the first recorded footprint around this dynamic new art form. From a historical perspective, we were the first country to have "a chainsaw in every home," so to speak. Lighter, one-man saws were developed here and people started to experiment with them, or "played around" might be a more accurate description, but eventually people realized that there might actually have been some money to be made at it.

Coupled with the fact that large-scale timbering was very much on the decline around this time, the humble little chainsaw soon found a new purpose.

Andreas Stihl is the German founder of one of the biggest equipment manufacturing companies in the world and early on recognized the marketing potential of carving with a chainsaw. Or perhaps he was simply intrigued and liked big wooden art. Either way, he brought over some American pioneers to help promote his product almost fifty years ago. Not long after that, some other carvers began traveling to Germany on a regular basis to do local contract work.

Around the same time, I had another friend who started traveling to Japan to teach chainsaw carving there as well. I used to make jokes about it: Jamie had Germany, Brian got Japan, and what about Joe? When does he get a country? I couldn't imagine it would actually happen someday, but then along came Russia.

Some of the guys there were just starting to dabble with chainsaw carving but not yet taking it very seriously. There were certainly no gatherings to speak of, and public demonstrations or festival-type events hadn't been conceived at that time.

Early on I met and connected with some guys at the university in Cheboksary who were also dabblers, and together we created the first "chainsaw carving symposium" at one of the city parks. It was a huge success and some of the attending carvers from other cities took the idea back home with them, so within a few short years there were carving events springing up all across the country.

I should mention that ice carving in Russia was already very popular at this time, but those guys were mostly working at night or ahead of time making the displays for various winter festivals and it hadn't yet been considered for public entertainment purposes.

We followed up with other events that were mostly held at the university and they became progressively more popular and better attended. For my part, other than a few master class lessons, most of the time was spent talking to television, magazine, and newspaper reporters as the "great visiting American artist." It was actually embarrassing at times, as some of the attending carvers were already showing signs of great talent and a couple of them would actually pass me in a few very short years, but there I was, getting all the attention.

One time during a ceremony, the city mayor was delivering his closing remarks and introduced me as the "greatest carver in the world." Later that day around twenty of us were gathered for a celebration dinner and I made the first toast, through a translator of course. I thanked everybody for their friendship and allowing me to participate (even though we were the organizers), and very much stressed that the mayor had misspoken: "I'm not the greatest carver in the world, just the luckiest."

There was another standing ovation, another round of vodka, and from then on I was truly just one of the guys. Plus another realization was just starting to settle in, in that very moment, Joe finally got his own country.

I haven't been able to participate in any of the events there recently but keep in touch with many of the carvers we started out with. From time to time one of them will mention about how I changed their life, not from any master class, but on the inspirational side by planting the seeds of possibility that made them think, "Hey, maybe I can do that too." I also remember in the early days when nobody signed their carvings. "Oh no," they would say, "only the masters do that." So I made a point to encourage them by explaining it another way: "Someday when *you* are the master, this simple carving from your early days will be a collector's item and more valuable, but only if it has your mark on it." It's true, and I think it worked as I notice most of them are signing now, which is a good thing.

Some of the carving festivals, competitions and symposiums around the world have risen to a level of excellence that nobody could have possibly imagined.

We have collectively pushed this fairly new art genre into a world-class industry of its own, and I am proud to have been a tiny part of that. Competitions, however, have taken over a large part of the festival scene in recent years and I understand that it does add an element of excitement, but I was already too far down a different path when this came about.

I am now considered one of the "old dogs" in the carving world. Thirty-two years have passed since the first time I picked up a saw with the purpose of turning a log into something else, and my best guess is to date I've completed somewhere close to five thousand in total. Along the way I have also discovered this unique community of free spirits and kindred souls, and like any modern dysfunctional family, love them or hate them- it is what it is, and we are all an inescapable part of it. There are so many other carvers out there now who have gone way beyond my skills (and imagination), some who I keep in regular contact with, and others I've yet to meet. One thing I am especially proud of is that we have forever changed the landscape of many age-old woodcarving traditions, and helped usher her into the modern era.

Медведям приглянулся парк

А. ОЛЕНОВА

Отдыхающие в парке 500-летия Чебоксар стали свидетелями уникального события. Прямо на их глазах огромный старый тополь, который предполагалось спилить, превращался в деревянную скульптуру. Композиция незатейлива: семья медведей на прогулке. Мать-медведица приготовила на обед бочку с медом, отец следит, чтобы два малыша не слишком шалили.

Bears in the park, Cheboksary Russia.

Twelve

Airports …

In the early years of commercial flight, the old turboprop planes were still in regular use and jet engines were only found on the bigger planes. Some of the old turbos had been in service for many years already and most of them looked like it, but it was the true beginnings of modern regional access. Some of them, most actually, were quite noisy, drafty and bouncy, but extremely reliable and got the job done with minimal drama. One time partway into the flight I noticed daylight coming through a big crack in the main cabin door and brought this to the flight attendant's attention. She glanced over, winked at me and said, "Thanks hon, just tell me if it gets any worse."

On another occasion, and a similar model plane in Canada, it was snowing so hard I thought we were going to hit the plow trucks that were making one final swipe so we could take off, so I asked the flight attendant, "Does this ever bother you?" "Oh no," she cheerfully responded, "we prefer this type of plane, it does really good in the snow."

I was a smoker for many years, not anymore, but some stories still revolve around this disgusting old habit. For example, one time I was surprised to find a smoking lounge in the Sheremetyevo airport since most airports today have more doggie-poo rooms than designated smoking areas. They are pretty nasty in general, but this one in particular felt like walking into purgatory. The glassed-in walls were located right in the middle of a boarding area, and already covered in a thick, gray film, like a giant smudge mark right in the middle of everything.

It was a place where only the bravest or most desperate would enter, and I was both. Surprisingly, it wasn't very crowded and I met an interesting fellow who also had some time to kill, so we struck up a conversation. Chatting up a complete stranger is something I'm quite good at actually, a skill passed on from my father. This guy had kind of an aloof Continental look so it was hard to guess his age, and said that he worked for some type of public aid agency in one of the Stans (Tatarstan, Kyrgyzstan, Uzbekistan, etc.). Looking back, I'm pretty sure he was some sort of a spook (foreign spy), but no matter, we immediately hit it off while sharing funny airport stories and waiting for our respective flights, just a couple of regular guys choking away in smoky glass aquarium-shaped room, in the middle of an airport.

Returning home from this particular trip, I had a connecting flight in Atlanta after arriving back in the States, and several international flights had come in around the same time so there was a big mess going through immigration and customs. I had plenty of time for the connection and luckily so as the entire area had bottlenecked like a salmon run gone bad. In particular it was the spot for collecting declaration forms listing what (if anything) we were bringing into the country that needed to be declared. It was really kind of redundant since the red gate was for taxable merchandise, the green gate was duty free and mostly for tourists like me with nothing but dirty clothes and souvenirs, and nothing of value to declare, so it didn't make sense as we were already past that point. I would guess somewhere close to a thousand people backed up and started funneling through.

The little man taking our cards was going as fast as he could without even looking at them, or the person handing it to him. I had just struck up a conversation with a couple of British guys in front of me and we started telling airport jokes while trying to make light of the situation. Eventually it was my turn to go through, I handed my card over and got about three steps when I heard him yell, "HEY, WHAT'S IN THE BAG?" The big, long line abruptly came to a stop and I couldn't imagine it was me, but sure enough when I turned around he was glaring right at me.

I should explain, this time I was pretty loaded down with a big suitcase, a large-wheeled duffel bag, my backpack over the shoulder, and a fairly large and colorful carry-on plastic shopping bag. Pretty much the most one person can manage by himself through an airport. (without a cart) In the carry-on bag were two big boxes of *Karukas*, my favorite Russian cookies that my future mother-in-law had given me just before leaving, and although I could have probably found room in the big suitcase, I didn't want to take a chance of them getting smashed and opted for an extra carry-on.

The big, noisy room suddenly fell quiet and I could feel hundreds of eyes on me; the troublemaker. Moments like that require great diplomacy, so I glared at the card collector and in my best and most irritated voice growled back at him: "COOKIES."

This caught him off guard, and he floundered for a moment, not sure what to make of that, then after a slight pause finally said, "Okay, keep moving," and I thought, *What the heck just happened here?*

A short time later, I ran into the Brits again and one of them said, "Oh look – another bloody troublemaker!"

I guess that kind of knee-jerk reaction on my part stemmed from a similar incident that happened some years before during a flight connection in Philadelphia. I was returning home from England and waiting for my suitcase to show up in the recently opened new international terminal. It was big, nicely modern, and pretty much empty at that moment so I found a comfortable spot to sit and wait.

Anyone who's ever traveled across time zones understands how you can get a bit blinky at times when suddenly it's the next day, but it still feels like the day before. My friend Sputnik, from Australia, told me about a time when he literally missed his birthday because of that. He was flying back home from Los Angeles, leaving on the 10th, and with the big time change, plus crossing the international date line from the other side, he arrived back in Sydney on the 12th.

So here I was waiting and minding my own business, I happened to noticed two other people off to one side who were also waiting, and a large suitcase wrapped in a black plastic trash bag between them. One of them got up and left, and a couple minutes later the other one also left, but neither one came back for the suspicious-looking package and my radar started to beep. Keeping in mind this was just a couple years after the 9/11 attacks and most airports were still broadcasting precautionary advice over and over to report any suspicious behavior and/or unattended luggage.

I found the nearest security person to alert him and he cut me off mid-sentence, pointed (without even looking at me) and said, "Go this way."

I tried to explain, "Sorry I know, but there's a suspicious—" and he cut me off again and said, "You go this way."

"Sir, very respectfully," I said, "I want to report–" He then cut me off a third time and said, "What's your problem, buddy?"

I snapped, and sorry, please don't judge me here, it could happen to almost anyone after sleep deprivation, not to mention I was still a wee bit foggy from the farewell party our friends had put on the night before. So I growled back, "What's your f 'n problem, buddy?" knowing full well that I was probably going to miss my connection for this one little weak moment in judgment.

Sure enough, two more guards came over and took me to a special security room. They started asking me questions while going through my backpack when another guy with a red coat came in who was obviously a supervisor. After getting drilled with a dozen more questions, I was reprimanded for speaking to an airport security officer like that. It's punishable under federal law, don't you know?

Finally Mr. Redcoat pushed my backpack over and said I could go, but by this point I was now wide awake and had enough of being treated like a naughty little schoolboy, and spoke up; "Hey guys, we're not the enemy here, the intercom is blasting away every two minutes to report any suspicious activity, so what about the suspicious looking package I was trying to report?

Old 'turbo-prop' planes, and a flat tire in Atlanta.

At that point I was too tired to care, but finally awake enough to go on the offensive, and speaking directly to Mr. Redcoat, I went through the incident from the beginning: "I was sitting there minding my own business, listening to the 'report any suspicious packages' announcements, when I noticed a suspicious-looking package and was simply trying to report it."

After a few additional stern words, he finally pushed my backpack across the table and said, "You can go now." Inside I was about to boil over but this time kept my cool, sitting there for a minute in disbelief, I finally growled back again, "Hey guys, what about the suspicious-looking package, huh?"

Finally Mr. Redcoat, looking a bit embarrassed I might add, explained that there was a leak in the new terminal roof so they had a container to catch the drip, and covered it up with a large garbage bag when it wasn't leaking.

It suddenly occurred to me what was happening here; apparently I wasn't the first one to report it and the normal security people were getting tired of explaining that to everybody. I just shook my head in dis-belief and couldn't get out of there fast enough, and luckily ended-up still making my connection in time.

You're bound to see some crazy things if you spend enough time in airports, I suppose, or maybe they just follow me around and I really am a bloody troublemaker? One time I was waiting for Nelli in the Pittsburgh airport, it was later on at night and she had been away visiting her mom (and daughter) for the past two months, so we were both pretty excited. This happened around mid-March of 2020 and the Covid pandemic was just kicking in, claiming Italy as its first casualty which is relevant to this particular story.

We always meet by the baggage claim area where on one side there is a big escalator to bring arriving passengers down, and on the other side another set of escalators leading up to the parking lot, where I normally stand and wait. This particular night I noticed an older couple trying to negotiate large suitcases onto the exit escalator and thought, *Jeez, why don't they use the elevator?* The man stepped on first but the lady was having some difficulty, and just as I was about to go over and help she finally got on as well. A big lady with a big suitcase and jet-lag was my fleeting observation.

At the same time people were coming down from the arrivals but no Nelli yet. I happened to glance back at the escalator just in time to see the lady fall over completely backward and land headfirst, face-up, on the moving metal stairs. She hit really hard and it was painful to even watch, but the escalator stopped immediately so she was close to the bottom and I rushed right over. I was the first person there as her partner was above and blocked by the two big suitcases and could only look helplessly on. Her head was bent backward and hanging down over the metal edge, so the first thing I did was put my hands under her neck and head and slowly straighten her out a bit, but ever so slowly and aware that there might be severe damage.

Almost immediately her eyes fluttered open and she was responsive, but confused about what had just happened, and immediately thankful I was there to help. I continued to hold her head as straight and comfortable as possible until help arrived, which seemed to take forever. Then she began to drift in and out of unconsciousness so I started asking her questions to keep her awake, also aware that she might have a concussion as well.

"Oh, where are you from? How was the flight? Where you coming from?" Things like that, and it worked. She seemed to perk up a bit and said they had connected in Atlanta and were returning from Italy. "We had to leave early, something's going on there," she said.

For the next ten minutes or so, our faces were around ten inches apart from the position I was holding her in so we were basically breathing each other's breath, and I had a fleeting thought: Well, *If she got it, I got it too...*

But honestly, it was very fleeting and I didn't, nor would I ever hesitate in any situation to jump in and help someone when it's necessary. Surprisingly, this wasn't the first or only time I happened to find myself in a situation like this, and I'm thankful to be blessed with good natural instincts. Time takes on a different dimension when you're holding someone who's badly hurt in your arms, regardless of whether you know them or not, but I'm side-tracking here.

At some point I suddenly remembered Nelli and why I was here, and glancing back over towards the other escalator- there she was! I saw her looking on with some others, and slowly shaking her head in bewilderment like *what the heck's going on here?* Just then a young airport security worker came over and got in position on the other side of the lady, looked me right in the eye and said something like, "Oh my God, I'm not trained for this, what should we do?" I suggested using her radio to call for help (yikes), and eventually others came and took over so Nelli and I could find her suitcase and get the heck out of there.

Just before leaving, however, I saw her again by the elevator, in a wheelchair and surrounded by paramedics and she recognized me right away, so I pushed my way through and asked how she felt. She grabbed my arm, pulled me in close and whispered, "Thank you."

One time on a 'red-eye flight' from the West Coast to Pittsburgh I had some personal mid-flight drama of my own. Returning from a three-week stretch of carving in Alaska, and part way into the five-hour flight, my leg decided to cramp.

At this particular time I was a couple years out from back surgery and things were pretty good, I felt strong again but every once in a while severe leg cramps were still happening. (Sciatica) They were absolutely unpredictable and hurt like hell. This time I was lucky that it was a red-eye flight, the plane was dark and most of the other people were sleeping. This was helpful to not look so creepy while I dragged my dead leg up and down the aisle like some character in an old horror film, which is basically what I was doing.

I remember it was a really long plane (extended cabin-type), and the flight attendants were all back in the rear cabin, so I made a point to hobble over in case they started to get suspicious about someone doing laps around the plane. They hadn't so far, but one of the women said she was a part-time massage therapist and started asking me questions about the cramp. The next thing you know I was face down on the cabin floor while she went to work on my leg and actually fixed it in short order, quite unexpectedly at thirty-five thousand feet above the ground, and can you imagine that?

Another time we were flying from Frankfurt, Germany to Moscow on "S-7," or Siberian Airlines, which was one of the bigger Russian/European carriers. It was a short three-hour flight, but bad weather forced us to go around the storms and took a bit longer that time. Russians take things very literally sometimes, especially transportation or other related official recommendations.

For example, when the seatbelt light went on everybody buckled up, and when the light went off, everybody unbuckled.

If the light came back on, they buckled up again, and you get the picture, it was really quite amusing.

We were flying through a heavy rainstorm with gusty winds and getting bounced around a good bit, but it was a brand-new Airbus 320, so I wasn't particularly concerned, and then they turned the landing lights on. I should mention that Siberian Airlines has a unique paint job on their planes. It's kind of a lime green like the old "Mr. Yuk" labels people put on medicine cabinets years ago, and a big sexy flight attendant cartoon lady painted on the tail section. With the combination of heavy rain bouncing off the lime-green fuselage it, had a bit of a kaleidoscope effect, plus bouncing around in both directions gave it a surreal and almost psychedelic feeling.

I remember when I was young and first started flying, people would clap when the plane landed, especially when it was a vacation island or someplace fun. Well sometimes they still clap in Russia, and this time it was a standing ovation.

Boeing 777-300ER, four hundred passengers plus twenty crew. It's a ten hour flight from New York to Moscow, plus an eight hour time change so you arrive the next day.

Thirteen

A Day in the Life …

A man came to the studio one day to ask questions and get information about having a bear carved into his old maple tree, so I explained the process, and asked him to send me some photos and said we'd go from there. Several months went by before I heard back, almost a year actually and one day out of the clear blue he called to see if I could come over and do it that Saturday. It was already Thursday and I politely said no, sorry. It was too short notice and I already had plans. But he continued by first apologizing, then explained that his wife was going out of town that weekend and he wanted it to be a surprise. Plus he was also willing to pay extra. I actually didn't have plans and agreed to do it, and possibly take him up on the offer to pay extra.

It was very early morning when I arrived, and just as I pulled up to the house the back door swung open and two big dogs came charging out at full speed, barking their heads off. I hollered out, "Dogs OK?" "Yeah, yeah," he said, so I slowly extended a closed hand and the biggest one lunged through the air and tried to bite it off, which I barely avoided. "No, no, not that one," he hollered back, and that was our first meeting.

Around mid-morning I took a short break to have coffee and a PB+J sandwich (peanut butter and jelly), and bandage my hand. I had just fallen off the ladder and landed fist-first on my biggest chainsaw (which thankfully wasn't running at that moment), but as luck would have it, my knuckles hit first, slicing four of them open.

The first part of my break was spent taking care of that. It wasn't serious enough for a hospital run but was a bit of a mess all the same, and of course I knew what to do. I was a long time professional at hurting myself and well-practiced in personal triage. Just as I was almost finished taping them up, the owner came over to join me for the break. He noticed the blood but didn't say anything, and I didn't offer an explanation.

We started talking and I made a comment about how nice it was to surprise for his wife. He looked at me like I was crazy and said, "Oh no, you don't understand; she didn't want this so I had to wait until she wasn't here." It was around this time my cuckoo clock alarm started going off, but everything turned out okay and at the end I went ahead and let him pay extra.

Working with a chainsaw does have an element of risk, but there are certain safety procedures that can very much reduce the chance of anything bad happening. Working on scaffold and ladders, however, opens up a whole different realm of dangers, but I'm especially careful and have been lucky in that sense as well.

The only other noteworthy injury happened while I was carving at a summer home in a fairly remote area, and I was the only one around that particular day. Around mid-morning, and just as I was taking off the final big chunk of wood before starting on the finish cuts, I lost control of it at the last second. It was a heavy wedge-shaped piece and knocked my scaffold plank off to the side when it slid down the wrong way. In less than a heartbeat, everything went out from under me and down I went.

Unfortunately I landed on my head and lost consciousness for a couple minutes, then slowly came around to find a mouth full of blood. Slowly I began moving my fingers around—all still there—then toes, arms, etc., and everything seemed to be working, so I slowly got up and made my way over to the van for some personal triage.

It turned out that the blood had come from a small cut on my forehead, but was everywhere. If you've ever had a facial injury you might recall the amazing amount of blood that comes from even the smallest cut, or at least it seems to be way, more so than other places. Just as I was icing the big lump on the top of my head and still cleaning blood from my face, the one and only car I had seen all day chose that exact moment to go by. The people waved, and I waved back very discreetly, trying to hide my bloody face, when all of a sudden they hit the brakes and came running over to see if I was okay. I instantly downplayed the situation and assured them everything *was* okay, but thanked them for stopping and insisted I was all good.

A couple of days later the owners invited us over for their "christening party" and it was actually the first time I had met them in person. There were probably around twenty or so people already there when we arrived, and it was all very enjoyable until the owner decided to take me around for personal introductions. The response each time was almost identical: "Oh, you're the artist; great job, we love it. And oh my God, we heard you fell off the scaffold?" So much for being discreet! I learned a valuable lesson that day: Unless it's Halloween, you're not fooling anybody when it comes to a bloody face.

Later on that summer I had a commission for St. Nicholas Alzheimer Resort in East Pittsburgh. The owner was an extremely nice and somewhat jovial fellow, and told me how they came up with the name: "Every day can be Christmas, because one day is about as far back as anyone that lives here can remember," he explained.

It was a fun carving and he asked if I was able to deliver it as well. So I loaded up old St. Nick and found the place early one morning. They had a spot already prepared so it didn't take very long to set in it place, but just as I was getting ready to leave he asked me to come with him, as there was something he wanted to show me.

The building was an old schoolhouse, very similar to the one I had attended as a child, so I followed him down the big hallway, up the stairs and into a smaller room that obviously had been converted into a casual lounge for the tenants. Along the way he also explained that when people moved in it was pretty much their last stop in life, so they were permitted to bring their favorite personal items with them; anything but a pet.

The room was almost empty except for one guy in a lounge chair with a television blasting away, and over in the corner was a fairly large chainsaw-carved eagle that I instantly recognized as one of mine. Right after opening my old studio someone had brought me a big load of tulip poplar logs and very soon I discovered they were prone to massive cracking and immediately stopped using poplar altogether, but somehow some of them had obviously survived. He went on to explain how it was a big hit with all the tenants and some of them would bring their visitors up to see it as well. Somehow he had guessed it was mine.

It was around this time I had another spur-of-the-moment request when a young guy stopped by to see if I could carve an apple into an old apple tree stump at his grandparent's farm the next day. He was home on a break from college and a few family members were getting together to celebrate something or other, plus he was on a pretty strict budget (he actually named the price), so I agreed.

I never really did find out what they were celebrating, but at some point it was just him and I sitting beside the old apple stump and he told me a story.

His pap had actually planted the tree shortly after buying the farm so many years before, and his fondest childhood memories were sitting together under it on hot summer days while "Pap" peeled apples for him and his other siblings and told them stories, or "spinning yarns" as they used to say. He couldn't specifically remember any of them, but was devastated when the tree died and they were going to cut it down for firewood. Pap was gone, and now the tree was gone, but not entirely, so we gave it a second chance at life.

It was truly a year for "last-minute" stories and another one came along which was very special. It began when a lady called on short notice. It happened to be Easter weekend and she wondered if I could schedule it for that Saturday. We had communicated some time earlier, but this time I did actually have plans for the weekend and said no. She apologized for asking on such short notice and explained that it was a spur-of-the-moment gathering at her brother's house and went on to explain the situation.

She said he was a really good guy, but had had some hard times lately, and she wanted to do something special for the family, and "I'll pay extra," so I agreed. Some other family members had arrived before me and right off I got the feeling that they hadn't all been together for a while, so I asked the lady who hired me about that. She explained the whole terrible story in great detail: They had all been on vacation somewhere, her brother, his wife and two young daughters, and the wife got sick with some kind of nasty rare flu virus. Her condition deteriorated rapidly so they cut the trip short, and two days later she was in a coma. Eventually she regained consciousness but was in an almost completely vegetative state, not even able to talk or even sit up on her own.

Eventually they brought her out and it was such a sad situation. She could look around, but was completely unable to communicate, and now her body was starting to curl up in a semi-fetal position. Part way through the day I took a break and sat beside her on the swing for a while, held her hand, and softly explained how I learned to do this.

At some point I went into the house to use the bathroom and there were photos covering almost every wall: at the beach, on ski trips to Colorado, and things like that, and what a beautiful woman she had been. I recognized a few of the places and talked to her about them, mentioning that we had been to some of them as well. I told her about my family and which place was our favorite, and what beautiful daughters and wonderful family she had.

It could have been my imagination, but I sensed that she was still "in there" and on some level could understand what I was saying. She actually squeezed my hand ever so slightly, and it was affirmed; part of this girl was still alive inside and it must have been pure hell to be trapped in that broken body.

After I was finished with the tree and packing up to leave, the sister came over to pay me and I got the biggest hug. She thanked me over and over and said, "It was the most fun day they've had in a long time," then gave me another big hug.

I think we've all have a profound experience at some time or other, the kind where it really hits home how fortunate and blessed we are to have a relatively normal life, and this was certainly one of those occasions.

One other quick example here: I had a commission for a lady who owned a hunting cabin on the shore of Lake Superior, which had originally belonged to her husband who had recently passed away. He was a prolific sport fisherman, and she always joked about having a statue of him carved into the giant Hemlock that was right next to the cabin. I'd actually worked on similar projects to this in the past, like the Mulligan story; it's always challenging, but also very rewarding. It was a lovely place, very remote and pristine, and the only downside was the early arrival of the dreaded "black flies of the north." This is something you have to experience firsthand to fully appreciate, for lack of a better description. Without a bug screen you have to keep your mouth closed or risk swallowing a few with each breath…

Fourteen

Carverdude …

The Internet came on pretty fast in retrospect; one day nobody had it and the next thing you know everybody and their brother was "online." My very first personal email address was "carverdude@aol" and the name stuck. Pretty soon everybody was calling me Carverdude, including my kids, girlfriend, even my own mother. One day I pulled into a customer's driveway and heard their daughter yelling down to the parents, "Mommy- the Carverdude's here."

Sorry to be a name-dropper, but have you ever heard of Pete Best? He was the original drummer for the Beatles, but was soon replaced by Ringo Star and the explanation at the time was that Pete was a virtuoso, whereas Ringo had more of a "bricklayer" style which was better suited to George and Paul's liking. I think there might have been some other issues, but it's an interesting point and translates into the carving realm as well.

For example, I consider myself more on the bricklayer side; lay down a few rows, stand back and have a look, then go back in and throw down a few more rows and pretty soon its way up to here- a big, good-looking wall. A lot of carvers work this way, but I also know some who have never seen "the wall," so to speak. They come at it from such a completely opposite way of thinking which always amazes me, and sometimes I do get a little jealous because it's everything I'm not, but wish to be.

These very simple but fundamentally different perspectives, however, take us all in different directions that can go way beyond career options and oftentimes spill over into personal aspects of our life. On that front I'm not jealous of anybody.

I've had many opportunities to speak in front of groups about my carving and specifically what I do, plus I always include art as a career in general. I've come to enjoy this very much and was also a bit surprised to discover what a learning experience that teaching could be as well. Putting your thoughts into exact words is really quite a practiced skill, so different from actually doing the work itself and this, in turn, forces us to articulate a somewhat subconscious behavior.

Add to that a roomful of complete strangers and it can be a bit daunting, but early on I developed talking points that were helpful to this end and the Pete Best story is a good example of that.

Sometimes I would use analogies and explain how for every famous artist or musician you know of, there are hundreds or possibly a thousand others doing exactly the same thing, but never quite make it to the top. They are, however, making a good living by doing something they love, and the old adage- "do it for love, and the money will follow" holds true more often than not. I was taught from an early age that art, music, and science were all well and good, but someday you need to grow up and get a real job, and like many others I eventually chose a different path.

Festivals are a big part of many freelance careers like mine, and in the early years almost every weekend from May until October would find me setting up at one of them, some close, some not so close, and the bigger the better. I discovered early on that answering questions or simply talking to people in general was an important part of it, possibly even more so than the actual demonstration side. Generally speaking, the same handful of questions came up time and again and the most common was, "How'd you ever get started doing this?" Tongue in cheek, I would explain how I hated my old job so much, couldn't take it anymore so I just bought a couple chainsaws and quit my real job.

Or, "Can you carve a statue of my husband here?" "No, ma'am," I would start out, shaking my head slowly from side to side and try to look serious, "we generally don't get logs that big."

Or my all-time favorite: "Wow, you must have a lot of patience to do this."

Seriously? I'm using a chainsaw to carve small wooden objects with a machine that is basically a small two-cycle motorcycle engine connected to a bicycle chain with a hundred sharp little chisel teeth and spinning around at an extremely high speed. Most of the time I'm chewing on a stick of gum, tapping my foot to some music wired into my headphones from an I-pod, (ear protection) and if there is anything more un-patient than that please don't tell me..

But we also learn early on when it's appropriate to joke around, and when it's better to hold back and get serious for a couple minutes. After awhile it actually becomes second nature and I've come to enjoy this side of performing in public, meeting new and different people from all walks of life.

Regardless of big or small, most festivals can and normally do include some long grueling days, especially when they're a week or more long and you're committed to a rigid schedule. But like I always say, it's amazing what we can tolerate when there's money connected to it!) Certain shows were well established and long-running, so many of the demonstrating artists like myself would return year after year and some of us would become good friends over time. 'Sugarloaf Art and Craft Festivals' in the Washington, DC, area were pretty solid, always interesting and a good place to do business as well.

Our little core group of demonstrators was often taped for promotional purposes such as live radio or television interviews, which on the surface sounds like fun, but they had a dark side as well.

Sometimes they took place around six in the morning and that was a bit of a stretch on occasion. Each day my buddies and I would start out by making a responsible plan to turn in early and rest up for the following day, and each night we would forget about that and stay out too late, again. Hold that thought-

An interesting thing I came to learn was that live television interviews were much easier than prerecorded spots. Filming ahead of time sometimes involves second and third takes whereas live only gets one shot, and once you get your head wrapped around that it really is much simpler. I would normally 'Hollywood-up' a bit and wear something more respectable, nice jeans and a Stetson hat, then say a few words and blow some chips toward the camera. Four minutes later it was all over, but it was then 6:04 and the show didn't open until 10:00.

The second and most important lesson, however, is that it probably is better to turn in early and be fresh for a live morning television interview, especially in a place like Washington DC where a million people could be watching. Alas, my ten minutes of fame.

One time I called my girlfriend at five in the morning and told her that this might be a good time for me to step back a bit on these television interviews, you know, let some of these younger guys have a chance, what do *you* think? She said, and I remember exactly: "I think you should get your lame-ass out of bed and go promote your business." Okay right, this was probably a ten thousand dollars a minute advertising cost on the biggest network in the nation's capital, and today it's free...

The promoters had numerous art and craft shows around the East Coast and somewhat similar to the 'Living Heritage' festivals in England that I mentioned earlier. Many of them were running twice a year, and if one was so inclined they could center their entire business around it. It was also a great opportunity for aspiring freelancers like myself, but I chose to do only eight per year, four different shows running through the spring and autumn. I followed this routine for almost ten years and could fill chapters with other silly 'behind-the-scenes' stories from around this time, but there were also some amazing things happening here as well.

One day an older and somewhat quaint-looking guy was watching me demonstrate for a while and came right over to introduce himself when I stopped for a break. He was a photographer for the Smithsonian Institute and explained that the Air and Space Museum was putting together an exhibit of folk art related to the air and space industry, and asked if would possibly be interested in carving something for them. They would in turn buy it to use in a forthcoming book, plus it would be part of a nationwide traveling exhibition as well. The only stipulation was that they already had too many space shuttle items, so anything other than that would be great. This was a big deal for a little carver like me, any carver actually, so later that day I consulted with my friends (the potter-dudes from Minnesota) for help with an idea. Without blinking an eye one of them said, "Buck Rogers," and that was it. In the very early days of television shows it was one of the most popular ones.

A black-and-white film with primitive graphics depicting a cigar-shaped rocket ship with sparks coming out the back while flying through space; classic material, and the museum loved it.

On further communication with the photographer, I pressed him with a burning question about an ongoing debate among many chainsaw carvers at the time. How can sculpting trees with a machine ever be considered folk art? What comes to mind for most people I think, is some lady in a long dress weaving baskets from swamp reeds, the husband outside splitting birchwood into shingles or beaver traps while teaching their kids how to play on a homemade dulcimer. But a chainsaw?

It was quite simply he said, and went on to explain why, and also seemed a bit surprised that I didn't already know the answer. "This particular classification falls under any art or craft form specific to a certain region or indigenous group using tools and natural resources close to their domain and passed down from three or more generations." Simple as that. So somewhere in the bowels of the Smithsonian storage vaults, just like in an old Indiana Jones movie, is a little chainsaw-carved folk art rendition of a cheesy old Buck Rogers space movie, and how cool is that?

Later in the day I met up again with my "ceramic consultants" as they were planning their evening debauchery, but this time I declined. I said, "No, I'm going back to the room and get a good night's sleep for a change, and maybe you should consider doing the same?"

They all had a good laugh over that, but wished me good luck anyhow and I wandered back to the hotel. Somewhere around midnight fire alarms started going off just as I was falling asleep, and it was really awful. So I pulled some clothes on, grabbed my phone and headed out the door, then something suddenly occurred to me.

At this point in time I was averaging over sixty nights a year in hotels and had never heard a hotel fire alarm before. Imagine the loudest, worst, and most annoying sound you've ever heard in your life, multiply that by ten and you'll start to get the picture. Plus I already knew that the first thing they do in situations like that is immediately shut down all the elevators. I was on the eighth floor and thought, *oh man, what the heck?*

The first thing I saw when I opened the door was a lady directly across the hallway in the opposite room with a young kid clutching at her dress. She looked distraught, so I tried to calm her down a bit and said, " Oh don't worry, it's probably just a false alarm," and I honestly believed that was the case.

Still, however, we could plainly hear fire trucks blaring away and saw the parking lot already filling up with people. In a half pleading voice, and almost in tears she responded, "No, you don't understand, my son just pulled the alarm. What should I do?"

Glancing off to the side I suddenly noticed a hallway fire alarm device in the pulled-down position, and could already hear people charging up the fire escape stairway to find the problem. It was instantly apparent what had happened; she had let her young child wander off alone to find a vending machine in a huge metropolitan hotel, and he got curious.

I smiled and suggested that everything will be okay, just go back inside the room and beat the child.

Yes, I know, what a terrible thing to say, but it was thirty years ago and dark humor was still somewhat in fashion. More importantly, I could see in her eyes that she got my message; there are far worse things that can happen to unattended children in places like this.

At that moment the stairway door burst open and two completely out of breath hotel guys came rushing out and instantly realized the problem. I politely excused myself and crawled back into bed, questioning my responsible decision to do the right thing by staying in that night. No good deed goes un-punished, eh?

Another somewhat chaotic incident happened the following morning as I was leaving for the show, and this time it was my bad. I would normally bring a large cooler along packed with ice and bottled water to share with friends and fair ground workers for the long, busy days. These guys always look after me, and although it was such a small gesture, it was always appreciated, especially when things got crazy/busy like they normally did.

It would take around ten pounds of ice to get through a good-long hot day, and rather than stopping somewhere to buy some I just filled a big bag from the hotel machines and save a couple bucks. Pretty clever, eh?

That particular morning the bag decided to break halfway through the main lobby which had smooth, shiny marble floors, and people everywhere. Ice cubes shot-out in every direction like a thousand little out of control hockey pucks. In an instant they were bouncing off of chairs, counters, people, and pretty much everything in the general area.

And it happened so fast there wasn't a thing I could do except just start looking around in bewilderment like everyone else with a *"hey what the heck, who is responsible for this big mess?"* expression. Then, of course, I got the heck out of there before anybody got suspicious.

A couple weeks later I was attending another Sugarloaf show in Manassas Virginia, which included a nice little carving job to do fairly close to the fairgrounds, so I combined them together to save some driving time. If the name Manassas rings a bell, it's probably because it was home to the second-bloodiest battle of the Civil War. The Clay Boys told me that they believed when something so terrible happened in a place like that, bad karma could be imprinted onto the very ground itself, and that's why they would never do that particular show. But I did, for a while.

They might have been onto something as some bad things did actually happen there over the years, and each time I would always stop at the Battlefield Park and say a small prayer. One bad weekend in particular, there was a woodturner who we all knew and very much liked that forgot his medicine and died of a heart attack right there on the fairgrounds while setting up his booth.

The following day, in the late evening actually, most of us were just winding down from the traditional Saturday night artist party when a small tornado hit. More specifically it was what they call a "microburst" and directly hit the enormous circus-type tent they had set up for vendors at the festival. There were a hundred ten-by-ten-foot booths inside and the storm leveled it, and most of those people lost almost everything. My display was right beside the tent but I was lucky and the physical damages were minimal.

It also turned out to be a close call for a handful of us who were fifty feet away sharing a box of wine in somebody's tent. It was actually a yurt, which is an authentic traditional Mongolian *ger* that nomads live in and belonged to a sport and adventure outfitter.

I've heard people describe tornados as being so loud it's like standing beside a freight train, and this is a fairly accurate description; you couldn't hear a thing above the noise. Lightning was crashing all around and the sky was totally lit up, almost like daytime, except the color was odd and reminded me of an old camera flashbulb with a slight blueish-tint. Suddenly my ears popped like a pressure drop when you're coming down in an airplane, and the yurt we were sitting in completely blew apart.

The owner had two Siberian huskies with him that didn't seem to mind this at all. I was hanging onto one of them, and he the other when he put his mouth against my ear and shouted: "Whoa that never happened before." Meanwhile, the small river of water crashing through the tent got deeper and the thunder got louder, but before too long we could tell that the storm center had passed, and we were spared.

Pretty soon a small army of fire trucks arrived to circle the area with additional lighting, and some of us started picking through the rubble. A torrential rain continued throughout the night which soon turned the entire place into a small lake as people started to gather and look on in dis-belief. It was too dangerous to enter any still-standing part of the tent, so I started pulling out some artwork from around the edges and made little piles of similar items, and pretty soon some others started to catch on to what I was doing and began helping.

Eventually we were able to salvage some of the mess and at some point I recognized someone I knew. He was on all fours, like me, pulling his artwork out of the water and when I got down to help him he actually smiled a wee bit and said, "God, I hate tearing down."

(Tearing down is festival jargon for packing everything up Sunday night so you could go home.)

I personally knew the promoters and sometime later in that hellish night I noticed them off to the side watching from their car, so I went over for a quick chat. The festival included over four hundred artists and a good many of them were unaffected, so I made a suggestion to go ahead and open the show as usual the following day. I said something like, "Please don't send these people home defeated by this." George looked up from his phone, winked and replied, "It'll be a cold day in hell before I ever cancel a show, Joe."

By morning the sunshine had returned and it was quite an amazing day. People pitched in like an Amish barn-raising and helped others sort things out, salvaging whatever they could from the disaster. Then I noticed something else; a metal artist I had briefly met once before was set up between a couple of the livestock buildings and I could tell right away she had been one of the tent vendors. I recognized the little fabricated birds, flowers, and animals as ones I had pulled from the wreckage the night before.

She said, "I couldn't believe it, I hadn't heard a thing about what happened and this morning when I got here everything was gone, but then I found all my things in a little pile, somebody must have done that during the night."

I didn't mention it was me, sometimes it's a nice enough feeling to do something nice and stay anonymous don't you think?

On this particular trip it was also the maiden voyage of my new 'show rig,' which I recently had re-painted to match a new trailer, sharp looking and very professional. The only thing I hadn't counted on was the extra weight and strain it would put on the van, but so far everything seemed okay. Part way home I was just starting up the mountain interstate highway and singing along with the radio. It was an old classic country song, "Six days on the road and I'm a gonna make it home tonight." All of a sudden I began to smell burning rubber and a quick glance in the rearview mirror confirmed it was me that was on fire. A thick plume of heavy black smoke was trailing behind me as far as I could see and kind of looked like images of the space shuttle going off, only sideways. (this is no exaggeration)

I whipped-off the road just in the nick of time before the entire front end burst into flames. Jumping out I soon found my little fire extinguisher, but it was a small one and pretty much useless. Then I remembered there was another bigger one somewhere in the trailer, but at the same time remembered my guitar was in the back of the van. It was my old favorite, been with me a long time and I normally didn't bring this one along for this very reason, so I had to make a split decision; save the van, or save the guitar? Maybe you can already guess what I decided on.

Have you ever been on a trip and suddenly noticed the highway is all scorched or stained from some terrible accident and wondered, *What the heck happened here?*

That was pretty much it, and surprisingly still noticeable even a year later

A short time later a flatbed tow truck pulled in to load me up, and I asked how much it was going to cost. The driver thought for a moment and said, "Sixty dollars to load it up, two dollars a mile after that, far as you want." I did a quick calculation and asked him if he knew where Pittsburgh was. He did, and I said "OK- drive-on brother," and off we went, but first stopping by the station to fuel-up, and also pick up his wife because she had never been to Pennsylvania before. (We were eighty miles from the border.)

Next came one last chapter to close-out the entire crazy week in Virginia. We picked up his wife at the station, who was anxiously waiting out front. She was a lovely, young, blonde girl and looked to be around nine months pregnant. And barefoot. (yes- absolutely I swear to God) She had a feisty little three-year-old boy and we all piled into the small cab, and off we went. Around five hours later I was back home again; me, one very dead van, and the trailer. But at some point along the way I got deeply into a 'whatever' moment and started humming the song again from when it all started, and they all knew the words and started singing along as well:

"Well I just passed a Jimmy and a White,
I been passing everything in sight,
Six days on the road and I'm a gonna make it home tonight …"

Fifteen

Fragments …

This last section includes a few random short stories that didn't quite fit into the other chapters. Some contain very personal information that is somewhat relevant to the complete picture, and a couple silly ones as well…

The Longest Elevator Ride …

"Excuse me, sir," a lady asked the hotel concierge with great concern in her voice, "if this elevator cable breaks will I go up or down?" To which he kindly replied, "Well, madam, it all depends on how you've lived your life." (It's my favorite joke.)

I too harbor some elevator reservations. Several years ago I was helping a friend build a new kiosk-type store located on the second floor of a local shopping mall. Across the hallway someone else was opening a new pet store around the same time and we were constantly bumping into each other in the freight elevator. Getting closer to opening day we began to notice posters with a photo of a baby tiger, and the text: "Bring your kids in for a picture of them holding a real tiger cub."

How cute, I remember thinking. *What will they think of next?*

Opening day came around, and everybody was extra busy busting through all the many last-minute details, and it was on my very last trip on the freight elevator when it happened; just as the doors were starting to close, I heard someone call out, "Hold the door please." So I hit the cancel button, the rusty old doors ground back open, and a man stepped in with a full-grown Bengal tiger on a leash. Let me say that again: a man walked in with a *Bengal tiger*. The doors closed and there we were, just the three of us: me, a complete stranger, and a full-grown Bengal tiger.

Did you know that there are well over a million elevators in the world? It's true, and nearly half are located in China, including one in Shanghai that currently holds the record for speed. It goes at over forty vertical miles per hour must feel more like a bullet train than an elevator ride, and I can hardly imagine the initial sensation of coming back down. Statistically speaking, elevators are twenty times safer than using an escalator, but there have been some pretty bizarre and terrible accidents over the years. Probably the most notable happened in 1945 when a B-52 bomber plane crashed into the eightieth floor of the Empire State Building. The subsequent collision smashed through the main elevator shaft and severed all the cables, in which is also the first of very few "free fall" incidents ever documented. Amazingly, one person survived due to the thousand and more feet of cable that had collected at the bottom of the shaft and cushioned the impact. Another bizarre footnote was one of the plane engines was later discovered at the bottom of another shaft.

Among the more colorful survivor stories happened in 2008 when a man was trapped for forty-one hours in a New York City office building. Working late one Friday evening he decided to step out for a cigarette, but the elevator jammed between floors and he was stuck there until Monday morning. Newspaper accounts at the time quoted him as saying, "I felt trapped like a rat."

The world record for being trapped, however, belongs to an eighty-five-year-old nun from a convent in Baltimore, Maryland. Sister Margaret Geary of Notre Dame de Namur was trapped for four days and three nights while her fellow sisters were out of town attending a conference.

She later recounted surviving on some celery sticks she happened to have in her pocket, prayer, and counting her blessings.

On the lighter side of elevator nostalgia, the famous Rising Tide Bar can be found on the world's largest cruise ship, *MS Oasis of the Seas*. Seating up to thirty-five people, the two-story lift takes around eight minutes, which allowed just enough time for one to enjoy a cocktail while making your way to the next bar.

Netflix has a hit television series called *The Tiger King*, where a crazy guy in Florida bred and raised tigers on a fairly large scale, and part of his business included sending them out for hire, so to speak. This practice was been stopped a number of years ago, but I'm certain that what I experienced back then was related. But really now, what are the chances of getting stuck in a six-by-six rusty old lift with one of them? Just me, a complete stranger, and a Bengal tiger spending a little time together, and you know how it feels in certain situations when time speeds up and slows down simultaneously? It was like that. A short, ten-second ride felt like an hour and I was already breaking out in a cold sweat the moment the doors closed. I thought, *Oh man, I should have used the stairs.* And of course I've heard the old adage, "You must never let an animal sense your fear," but we were way past that now; I was nearly paralyzed and on the verge of peeing myself.

The tiger, on the other hand, merely glanced impassively over and I have to say, what an incredibly beautiful animal.

My son had a chance to sit on Shamu the Killer Whale many years ago while visiting a Sea World park, but other than that, how often in real life do we get a chance to be so close to such an amazingly powerful and wild animal like that?

She was a big one too with huge paws, thick, bulging muscles, and shiny white canines, though I suddenly realized she didn't need teeth, or even claws for that matter; that girl could accidently break me in half.

Under different circumstances it might have been a more fun experience, but, no, strike that thought, from personal experience I can say for sure there is no way to have fun trapped in an elevator with a live tiger. After what seemed like an eternity, we all finally reached the top and went our separate ways, thus ending "the longest elevator ride."

"Don't be alarmed, folks. ... He's completely harmless unless something startles him."

Candyman …

St. Basil's Cathedral in Moscow is possibly the most photographed building in the world and you'll know why the first time you see it. Commissioned by Tsar Ivan IV, better known as "Ivan the Terrible," it was built to celebrate the conquest of Kazan, the Muslim capital of Tatarstan. Legend has it that Ivan subsequently had the architect's eyes put out so he could never again create something so beautiful. It's a great story but probably not true; he was quite well known at the time and went on to design other famous buildings after that, plus Ivan already had done some other pretty terrible things leading up to this point and probably didn't need to add to them, anyhow. But I tell you this, it is one of the most amazing buildings you'll ever see, and it is now a museum so you can explore almost every little magical inside corner.

Several years ago while on another trip to Russia, we had a spur-of-the-moment chance to visit Kazan. One of my wife's friends was a language professor at the university in Cheboksary and organized a trip for her foreign exchange student program. They had a couple extra seats and asked if we would like to go along. That particular group included a small cross section of nationalities including Swedes, Germans, a handful of Russians, and one American, counting me. It was to be a one-day excursion, leaving very early in the morning and returning late at the end of a very long day. We were completely exhausted by the end, but what an amazing day it was. We had the chance to explore an exotic ancient city with its Kremlin and several century-old churches and mosques, most with their doors open so people could go inside any time of day.

There were ethnic restaurants and exotic cafés around every corner, and it was such an amazingly vibrant city ensconced in ancient Eastern architecture with a very distinct hint of Arabian culture. But it's also way more than visual when you visit places like that for the first time; the colors were slightly unusual, and there were many new sounds and accents coming at me in every direction, along with so many different smells and aromas. As a result, it was nearly impossible to capture something like that in a photo (but we tried!), and how amazing is it when a certain smell can take you back to an exact moment in the past?

We all separated shortly after arriving with a plan to meet up later on in a certain area, which was an open-air café-type food court surrounded by well-preserved ancient Tatar architecture, but with a very old-world European ambient feeling. I made a point to join the three Swedish students, partly because they all spoke good English, but mainly because I was curious to ask why they chose Russia for their exchange country. The food selection was, of course, different and interesting, so naturally conversations turned to cuisine experiences around the world, good, safe common ground. They shared some nice stories about good and bad experiences, all in all a really pleasant conversation, until it was my turn.

For some unknown reason that still puzzles me, how this particular story popped into my head at that exact moment I'll never know. I had so many other interesting examples like pan-seared grouper in the Florida Keys, smoked salmon and halibut in Alaska, lobster bisque from the icy North Atlantic states, jambalaya and salsa cuisines both north and south of the Mexican border.

So many great North American culinary experiences, but instead here's what came out:

A couple longtime friends back in America had two young daughters, who I'd known since they were babies. We were part of a small, close-knit group of friends and all our families spent good amounts of time together with outdoor and adventure activities always on the front burner. The mom and dad were both what I lovingly refer to as "culinary health nuts," the exact opposite from me a "culinary low-flier," and we'd always had great fun poking at each other around that subject.

At breakfast time, for example, Ed had cereal nuts and berries, while Joe was on the other side frying up a pan of bacon. For an afternoon activity snack, Ed pulled out a whole-grain energy bar, while Joe, of course, finds a Snickers bar, and so it went, and the girls knew this too. I was the candy man, always ready with a bag of M&M's or Pixie Sticks, and various other popular sugar-infused products the girls would otherwise never have had a chance to try, but that's what candy men do. I never tried to hide it of course, in the mom and dad's eyes it was total corruption, but to their credit they never said a word. Pretty soon the girls came to expect it and believe me it wasn't an obsession on either part, just a silly game, so one night I made a joke: "Ed, these girls love me because I always bring them candy, and one day they'll forget why they love me – they'll just love me!"

That was my story and looking back maybe I could have chosen better. I was cracking myself up with an old party joke (and memory) and expecting everybody to laugh, but that didn't happen.

Up until this point they were pretty much engaged, hanging on every word actually, then I sensed a bit of confusion and their expressions suddenly soured. One of them finally spoke up collectively for all three. He began by slowly shaking his head in a most concerned manner, and finally pushed it out: "Wow, that is so American..."

To "buy love," I suppose is what they were thinking, but nothing could be farther from the truth and it was a real insight into the young Swedish mind. By this time I had completely forgotten to ask why they chose Russia for their exchange program, and I also have no doubt they shared this story of American opulence with many friends back home.

Our Kazan group.

St Basil Cathedral located in Red Square, Moscow.
One of the most photographed buildings in the world.

Bear Facts …

What would you guess to be the world record for carving the most bears in one hour? Here is the criteria: Carvers are supplied with eight-by-eight-inch-square blocks that are sixteen inches long, all identical, and they can have a helper to keep the saws gassed up while getting the next block ready.

You would be wrong if you guessed thirty-one as that was second place. First place, and the all-time record is thirty-nine.

One year at the Rendezvous a handful of us were gathered around a campfire at the end of a day and telling our respective bear stories. It's a bit of an industry inside joke because they are so much in demand that you can't get away from them, even if you wanted to.

Mick went first; he had gone to see a client in London who happened to own a big chain of nightclubs and was quite well off. *This is great*, he thought, *a chance to work on a real masterpiece*. But no, this guy wanted a bear. Mick hated making them more than anything else and was known for carving them in the throes of death; inside the jaws of a giant wrench, head chopped off by a guillotine, things like that. And if that wasn't bad enough, the owner ended up not liking it when he finished until he had a party the next day and all his friends liked it, so then he decided to like it too.

My incident started with an email from "the Pickle Doctor," which sat in my inbox for several days before I had the courage to open it.

It turned out the guy was a carpenter's helper on an enormous log cabin building project in Utah, and he was the only one on their crew with a computer. After some further communication I flew to Las Vegas, rented a car, and drove across the desert into Southern Utah to meet the owners. Their property bordered the northwest boundary of Zion National Park and was quite extensive. There were three mansion-sized houses, the new enormous log cabin (which was built to serve as a hunting trophy lodge), a full-time staff of housekeepers, maintenance workers, and some cowboys to run the ranch side of the estate. Real cowboys. Sometimes you can tell the difference between a millionaire and a billionaire, and these people were not millionaires. Someone later told me that the family owned a construction business and had built half of Las Vegas. But they were really nice people and we sat down together to look through my portfolio, studying each photo with great interest until the wife finally spoke-up and said: "We like bears."

Later on back at the campfire and after some beer and silliness started to kick in, a handful of us decided to pay tribute to the humble little bear. We each did a ten-minute "quick carve," piled them up all covered in flammable chainsaw oil, and put a match to it. Then we laughed and took pictures, it was really great fun.

One more little bear story while we're on the subject, well, two actually. We live in the foothills of the Appalachian Mountains in what they call the Laurel Highlands, appropriately named as mountain laurels abound here. One day Nelli heard our cat scratching at the back door but didn't see him and stepped outside to have a look. When she turned around there it was;

A bear cub sitting right there. She is admittedly a bit of a city girl and really didn't like it because even city girls know that the big mama bear was probably nearby.

Another time it was evening and I thought I heard a car in our driveway, but I did a quick check out the window and nobody was there. I was turning to walk away and suddenly had a thought: *No, I know I heard something.* So I looked again and there it was—a giant, full-grown black bear trying to rip open our trash can. This particular can was industrial size around four-feet tall, but still only came halfway up the side of Mr. Bear- so he was a good eight-footer. If that's hard to believe, keep in mind that the Pennsylvania state record was taken around twenty miles south of here and was 733 pounds.

We learned something about a bear's speed that day. I cracked the window to get a good photo and this giant bear hopped up the hillside faster than anything I'd ever seen move before, faster than a startled cat to give you some idea. Everybody knows you cannot outrun a bear and from what I observed, you're not even going to get three steps away.

Not Mr. Big, just a cub.

Jersey Girl …

Most of us have dear friends that help guide us, accept us as we are, and provide backup when we need it. They support our decisions, encourage creativity, and are reciprocally inspired by the friendship. They also learn from us, as we do from them, and this is my chance to mention one of my closest and most interesting longtime friends, Lauren. She is a professor of graphics and arts design by day, world traveler by past, and an ongoing bundle of full-on infectious creative energy on a daily basis.

We've been artisan friends and crossing paths for many years, which includes projects such as serving as president and vice president of the Craftsmen's Guild of Pittsburgh for seven years, installations at the Pittsburgh Center for the Arts, plus various other related art festival events in and around the city of Pittsburgh.

But first a brief description: tall, thin, blonde, kind of a California surfer girl look with a lingering New Jersey accent (and related slang). She sometimes lived abroad with her family as a child, then spent her early adult/post-college years living on a sailboat in the South Caribbean islands, which included a short stint as the "Jägermeister Girl" in a famous Martinique seaside café (worth honorable mention here, I think). Prior to that time she spent a few years living and working in Europe, starting in London, then spent another year living in the south of France, which is where one of my favorite Lauren stories occurred.

At some point she took a job working in an upscale resort as a chef's assistant, without understanding a word of French. As in much of Europe, one of the great delights of Mediterranean-style cuisine is where everything's made fresh daily, especially salad dressings, mustards, and various other sauces or condiments. Fresh mayonnaise is also very popular, and considered a staple actually, but apparently, and I've researched this a bit further, there is some old folklore related to having a woman in the kitchen at a particular time of month. (For example, menstruating women did not make butter, lest they ruin it). Her boss was an old believer who knew all about this, and after a frustrating exchange of words she finally realized what he was trying to ask when he took a white napkin and pulled it up tight between his legs: *is it your time?*

On a personal note, I cannot completely discount this old folklore based on a personal experience when I was still quite young. Some people I knew at the time lived on a farm and were having a big holiday party and within a minute of stepping out of the car, their normally calm pet cow charged my girlfriend. There was a bit of unexpected drama and confusion, of course, and later on she mentioned that it was her time of the month, and I'm certain the cow picked up on that. I also think that oftentimes we find a spot of truth in so many seemingly bizarre incidents and this crazed cow memory would have been long forgotten, if not for the French mayonnaise story.

Some years ago, around the time we first met, she had just returned from six months teaching at a woman's university in India, followed by a "father-daughter" excursion to Egypt, and was recovering from a bilateral mastectomy after a second round with breast cancer. In typical "full-on Lauren" fashion, this came along with more good stories. The night before surgery she had a "bye-bye boobies" party where everyone had to bring two of something and put it on the table. She also asked a mutual friend of ours, who was a very accomplished clay and ceramic artist, to cast a mold of her upper body for a possible "before and after" exhibition.

I wasn't around for that part, but our friend shared a full account with me later, and in great detail: "It wasn't easy, when she sat up, the clay wouldn't stick on the undersides, when she laid down everything went flat and was not at all the look we were after, so it took half the night, but eventually I worked it out and had a lot of fun trying." True to her word, she actually did create an exhibition, *Marking Time*, at Carnie Mellon University in Pittsburgh.

On a very personal side, I think something she wanted most in life was to have kids, at least one, and after several unsuccessful attempts she decided to try artificial insemination as a solo parent. Then breast cancer took away that option as well, so she began applying for adoption. The university where she teaches is a Catholic entity and very much involved in the regional "foster to adopt" program, but even that didn't work out for a couple years and she began to lose hope. Then one day out of the clear blue she called to say, "Hey, guess what? The agency just called and a baby is coming on Monday."

(And could I please come over and help with some little home improvements.) Never before had I seen someone so scared, happy, and excited all in the same moment. Then along came little Will who is now in his early teens at the time of this writing.

This is another close friend and prolific carver, 'Bob Shamey', who holds the world record for the most chain links carved into a toothpick. (17)

The Institute ...

TRI is an abbreviation for The Rehabilitation Institute, more commonly known as the Children's Institute of Pittsburgh. This is a large and very well-known hospital in the Squirrel Hill neighborhood, one of the best of its kind in the nation, and one day they called me about a possible carving project in the playground area. This particular playground was really quite unique as they had designed and built a wheel-chair accessible "treehouse" with swinging walkways leading to and from, and all around a massively big American Beech tree. It was a grand old tree for sure with large limbs extending under and over the walkways, and the design took advantage of the sloped property so that one side was ground level, then the opposite side projected out over the lower part of the property, which gave it a feeling of hanging in mid-air as well. It was such an overall cool design, but unfortunately they killed the tree while building the treehouse. (accidently of course) Right away I could see why; they had damaged the root structure with too many misplaced support posts. Older trees (like people too, I suppose) can sustain very little root damage at a mature age, and it's a fairly common mistake, but I also think this tree was very near its natural life end, anyhow.

My part would be to salvage something of the stump and transform the majestic remaining base into some natural setting-type critters like birds, little ground animals, or whatever else; they pretty much left that up to me. After some rounds of input and communication, we scheduled a starting date for immediately after the tree had been cut to size, and it was a very exciting project.

Like most big stumps, it required a bit of creative scaffolding, which sometimes took a fair amount of set-up time before the real work could begin.

During a lunch break on the first day I decided to check out their cafeteria and chose a time when I thought might have been more or less empty. I found a seat way over in the far corner in case someone else came in. Part way through the soup and sandwich special that day I noticed a large and somewhat uncoordinated group of kids coming in, and two of them came stomping straight toward me. It was perhaps not such a large group, just big in volume and as they got closer one of them blurted out, "Excuse me, you're in my seat."

Oh my gosh! I apologized immediately and quickly moved away as other kids of similar size and determination began to wander over as well. They were clearly some very special campers, so at the first available chance I pulled one of the staff members aside to ask about them. She explained they were kids with Prader Willi Syndrome. They had multiple issues and went there a few times a year for treatment, and sometimes the families attended as well, to get help with adjusting their home-life environment.

Some of the side effects included extreme eating disorders, small body extremities, incessant picking at their own skin (making scabs that sometimes never healed), IQs just slightly above or below autistic levels, plus a number of other issues.

I immediately noticed two other things: you couldn't begin to guess their age, and they all had precious little twinkle eyes that looked straight into you in a way that was so personal, and let you know that you had their complete and undivided attention.

Sometime during the second day I noticed them walking by my work area and some of them recognized me as well, and started waving, so the next day I joined them for lunch and explained what I was doing there. This was my first chance to see them up close and to be honest, some of them *were* really a mess, but now that the ice was broken, they started to open up and let me into their special little circle.

Later that day they came by my work area again so I took a chance and let them in. The entire playground area had been cordoned off and I was under strict orders not to let anybody in, it was a potentially serious professional blunder but that thought never occurred to me. This was a group of around ten or so and the playground had always been the highlight of their day so they were all immediately relieved to get back in, and even more curious about me, I suspect.

The therapists knew we were breaking some rules but were completely supportive nonetheless, and we were all having a great time together until the director happened to come by and see this happening.

The therapists and I started to cringe a bit until one of them (John Parker) stepped forward and told her, and I quote: "It's Doe Ding, we have lunch with him every day and he's our friend, it's OK."

And it was OK, even though, caught off guard a bit, the director rolled her eyes in disbelief and let us continue, and even came by for lunch with us one day (perhaps to watch us interact, I'm guessing).

By the end of the week we were old friends and strangely I was almost as excited to see them as they were me.

I should also mention something about my first experience with therapists in an intense environment like this: it takes a very special personality type that not only accepts the difficult conditions, but thrives on working with challenged people like that. My short time there created a space—or fun interruption might be a better description—for everybody to step outside their normal routine and make a new friend.

The director of the program had been away on holiday during this first week and the following Monday there was great excitement as they introduced me to "Dennifer." Right away I could tell she was clearly the band leader, and these were *her kids*, and who the heck was this "Doe Ding?"

It didn't take long to sort that out; she was a smart French American girl from northern Wisconsin with reddish-brown hair, a big bubbly smile and nice legs; the attraction was immediate. She was also somewhat astonished how an outsider like me had grown so close to the kids in only one week, and asked me on a date. It was a pre-planned excursion to a local farm, which included a pumpkin patch exploration and a long hayride through the cornfield, which all sounded like fun, so I instantly agreed. It was an interesting time to say the least.

First we had to get everyone on board the hay wagon, and keep in mind they were some big and somewhat uncoordinated kids who absolutely could not be rushed. I sat near the front of the wagon after loading up and as we were about to set off, I noticed the tractor driver looking a bit nervous, so I tried to reassure him that we were OK and that I would pay close attention.

He smiled back at me and said, "No, that's not it, I think we're going to need a bigger tractor."

After my work was finished at the institute I became a somewhat regular fixture there and also got involved in the annual "free care fund" without the slightest inkling at the time how that would play a part in my own life some years later. My donated carvings were an instant hit and soon became a much sought-after item in the following years to a point where I eventually became their biggest donor.

Several years later, my oldest son was in a terrible car accident, which required multiple surgeries, weeks in a trauma unit, then extensive rehabilitation that he didn't have the proper insurance to cover. Someone suggested that we apply for a free care grant at the institute, but he was twenty-two at the time and too old for a children's institute at this point, or so I thought. We did apply, and he was accepted, which was such amazing grace, and that place brought him back to full health not only physically, but mentally and spiritually as well.

There was also another equally amazing thing happened along the way; I discovered that the people who were making decisions on who qualified for eligibility were completely separate from the fundraising process and totally unaware that I was their biggest contributing donor at the time.

After this I became inspired to find more volunteer opportunities at other extended-care facilities after my experience at the Institute, which included a veteran's hospital, and a local county home for the aging. I had mixed results, but it is always interesting and rewarding as well.

I found that my biggest contribution in all of these places was the appreciation by the staff, and especially the many wonderful volunteers so crucial in this type of extended-care environment.

Sometimes while demonstrating there I would glance around and notice half of the elderly patients had fallen asleep while watching. They would be enjoying the warm sunshine and had. simply dozed off. You learn very early on not to have any expectations when donating your time for any type of volunteer situation; it's all part of the great circle of giving and one can only hope there are still people like that around when it's our time for the chair.

I haven't been back to the institute for a number of years now, but expect it is still more or less the same wonderful and caring place. My carving is long gone, and much of the staff I came to know have also rotated out, plus Dennifer and I, who dated for several years also parted ways, but I will always look back on that time with the fondest of memories.

"Chester"

Chester …

We had a pet bird in the old house named Chester, a small orange and white tame cockatiel and he was happiest to be sitting on somebody's shoulder. So happy that it got to the point where it became a nuisance at times. Then we discovered that Chester was actually a female when she laid her first egg one day.

We also had a crazy cat at the time and in the beginning it was a constant concern, wondering what would happen if we left them alone. Would he end up eating her? Eventually however, they became the best of friends and sometimes we would come home to find the cat sleeping inside the birdcage and Chester sleeping on the top, or sometimes both were inside together.

If you've ever raised an indoor bird before then you would already know that it was necessary to keep their wings trimmed back so they couldn't fly too fast and break their little neck by slamming into a window, so we were always careful about that and made sure she could still get around, but not too much.

So, one day I was in front of the stove boiling up a pot of water for the boys and myself, for our favorite dish: macaroni and cheese. At some point I heard the little girl flying across the room, which reminded me that she was overdue for a trimming, and then realized she was coming straight for me. I wasn't concerned, however; she would probably land on my shoulder and cuddle up under my hair, but instead she went right past me and fell into the pot of boiling water. I'm guessing it was the rising steam that lulled her into landing, or possibly disabled her natural lifting ability. Regardless of why, there she was in the pot.

After what seemed like eternity, but was probably only a second or two, I screamed and stuck my hand into the boiling water and scooped the poor thing out, relieved that she hadn't gone completely under. She was still very much alive, but I could see right away her little legs were badly burnt and knew that within a very short amount of time some of the skin would blister and fall away. I was in a panic and couldn't stand the thought of her burning, so I instantly put her under the cold-water spigot, which probably wasn't the best thing to do, but again I was in panic mode, and she survived.

I should back up a bit and explain why we had this bird in the first place; She was my "canary in a coal mine," so to speak. I was raising two boys at the time, mostly on my own and always worried about them missing out on a softer "women's touch," and this was my solution. I felt like it might help teach them to be gentler and if I ever came home one day to find a dead bird then there might be reason for concern. But that never happened, and in fact it was me that almost killed the poor little thing.

Fortunately I happened to be recovering from back surgery at the time and didn't have to miss any work, so for the next week or so I was able to stay home and nurse her back to health. This, however, wasn't quite as easy as it may sound. For starters, she developed a bad cold, which was probably the result of me holding her under cold water for too long, and her legs were a mess. I used antibiotic salve in the beginning to make sure she didn't get an infection, then switched to cortisone cream after a couple days to help regenerate the saggy, scarred skin still hanging from her tiny little legs.

She literally sat on my shoulder for five straight days snuggling up closer than ever to stay warm, and constantly shifting her weight from one leg to the other for relief. Pretty soon, and to our great relief she not only survived but was back to her own self in a fairly short amount of time.

A couple years later we put our house up for sale in order to move to the mountains and build a new one, and I knew that it wouldn't be possible to bring her along for this, so I put an ad in the paper. The asking price was two hundred dollars and the first lady who called asked me: why so much? She went on to say that the mall sold them for sixty, and the cages were fairly cheap as well.

I said it was a nice cage, and she was a really smart bird. (which wasn't exactly true) I also told her that she was as friendly as they came (very true) and that we love this bird and not giving her away to a free home or somebody looking for a good deal.

She said, "OK thanks, we'll come right over." I also made her promise that if things didn't work out to just call me and we'll take her back, no questions asked and happily refund the money, no questions asked. Then a couple days later she actually did call, but just to tell me everything was okay, they love her too and I could hear our little Chester chirping away in the background.

#1 son Jason, with "Shamu, the killer whale"

#2 son, David, with the author

#3 son, Aleks, with our mangy cat "Hoody"

Mallorca…

I mentioned my wife in the first chapter and decided to include a little story about how we met and ended up together. We both already had two kids of our own, plus a lot of history behind us by this point in our lives so we took it kind of slow in the beginning. We actually met on a Russian/Euro dating site around fourteen years ago (at the time of this writing) and after communicating for a while we agreed to meet somewhere with a nice beach for the first date. Mallorca Spain is an island which lies almost in the middle of the Mediterranean Sea, a quick one hour flight from Barcelona, and that's what we decided on. (her suggestion) By this time we had been communicating for a good while and already had a good feeling about each other, but still made resort arrangements so that in the un-likely event sparks didn't fly, we could still have a nice time together with the least amount of awkward moments. (my suggestion)

Let me back up for a moment in case you're wondering what goes through somebody's mind when they sign up for an overseas dating site. From my side, I had been single for a few years and tried a popular dating site here in America where I met a couple really nice girls, had some fun dates, but no sparks. One thing that always bothered me about this process was that you have to answer so many questions so specifically, and the one I always got hung up on was distance. It seemed like they were saying: closer range- less options, go farther- more better, so I completely removed myself from that from that part of the equation. Although I wasn't at all obsessed with the whole process of finding someone this way to begin with; it sure was interesting.

It's also interesting to note that even though a good many people at that time were starting to meet on-line, it was still information you didn't openly volunteer. This of course has dramatically changed and I'm remembering a specific and very short moment in time when it just started to become popular.

So back to Mallorca. (pronounced 'my-orca' by the way) According to our plan, she would already be there when I arrived, but the hotel clerk couldn't find her on the register. I was over the top excited by this point, but also feeling a bit fuzzy from some travel complications and had barely made it there on the right day due to a botched connection. (I have actually been a day late a couple other times for the exact same reason) Confusion set in, so I asked again in another way; "*Señor por favor*, please look again." He did, and slowly shaking his head in an apologetic manner came back and gave me the bad news; "*sorry, she's not here.*"

It was an hour shuttle ride from the airport to the resort and also a very hot day, steamy tropical hot, so at this moment I was feeling a bit like a drowned rat and politely excused myself to the rest rooms to pour some cold water over my head and collect my thoughts. Maybe she had been delayed like almost happened to me? The cold water helped, and coming back for the third round of asking I explained that she is Russian; and don't you have the passports? This time he came back with a big smile on his face; "*Hola Señor*, I have good news for you!" Ten minutes later she walked into the lobby and we met for the very first time, both in total amazement, and in case you're wondering- sparks!

Our resort was located in the village of Cala d'Or and turned out to be a perfect place to meet. They had a great beach that was surrounded by old Mediterranean style cafés, cobblestone streets lined with quaint little shops, and party lights hanging everywhere for the evening ambiance. We spent the days relaxing by the water and getting to know each other, and eventually exploring different interesting parts of the island. Neither one of us were strangers to traveling in Europe, her more than me actually, but this was something quite different than either one of us had experienced before. Plus her English was a bit limited at that time and my Russian was non-existent, but this only added to the mystique. Some of our dinner conversations would start out something like- "Pig, chicken, or fish?" In spite of that it all felt so perfectly natural and we were completely comfortable together from the very beginning. Two weeks flew by in a blink of an eye and all too soon it was time to say goodbye, so Nelli gave me her froggy ring and we promised to see each other again. It had been such a wonderful time but now it was over and we were both holding back the tears.

A short little side story to the ending; Sitting in front of the lobby and feeling a bit forlorn while waiting for the bus, I happened to notice a couple with two kids who were also waiting. They had a very specific Scottish accent I recognized so I made my way over to introduce myself and ask "where's home?" To make a long story short, they lived near the 'wee Shire of Moffat', and the dad not only knew my friend 'Chainsaw Pete' who lived nearby, they worked together and Peter was actually his boss. I thought; *what are the chances of this happening?*

Coming from America, waiting for a bus on an island in the Mediterranean Sea, and run into a friend of a close friend from Scotland. But I was already in a surreal state of mind by this point and just asked him to give him a kick in the leg from me when you get back; "Say it's from Joe," to which he laughed and agreed. A few days later I got a message from Peter; "Ouch ya bastard."

That was in July, and three months later I was on a Delta flight to Moscow for date #2.

On the Metro, first time in Moscow on date #2. Both very tired at this moment but also very happy.

Summary ...

I believe there are very few coincidences in life. There are some, of course, but way less than we imagine, and I am living proof of that. Like so many others, I was taught from an early age that we are all special, unique, each and every one of us is different, like a snowflake, but as time went along it began to feel more and more like we were all pretty much the same. Some excelled while others didn't, while some got lucky and some didn't, plus we are all supposedly a product of our own environment and much of it is already laid out in the cards, right?

But eventually I snapped out of that thinking and realized there is way more to it than we realize. For example, some believe that luck is a planned event where preparation meets opportunity, and I completely agree with that. But sometimes we do just get lucky, and I think my life falls somewhere in-between.

My first serious girlfriend in high school lived a few towns over in the big city of Greensburg, and sometimes I could "hop a train," which, of course, is very much different than buying a ticket and following normal boarding procedures. We would simply grab onto the side of a car as it went by and hang on. Normally they ran earlier in the day so hitchhiking was the second best option, and still ten times better than walking the entire way. Either method still involved a fairly long walk through town and each time I would pass by an art museum in an old majestic stone mansion on North Main Street.

I can't remember exactly why, perhaps to get out of the sun for a couple minutes, or maybe find a restroom, or most likely out of curiosity, I went in one day to have a look around. At first glance it was nice but seemingly normal, but on the second floor and prominently placed on a marble column I discovered a cement perching eagle that would change my life. It was the first-time art would "speak to me," as they say.

It wasn't until many years later that I realized the importance of this chance encounter, but in this moment I remember staring in awe and wondering, who made this magnificent sculpture? Where were they now, and were they even still alive? Most of all, I wondered how someone ever got to that level of skill and talent to make something so wonderful.

Many years later after I had been carving eagles for a living for some time (among other things, of course), I suddenly came to realize the true power of dreams and how they can manifest themselves into the deepest part of our subconsciousness and guide our destinies. Some people are blessed with a great natural talent, but others not as much, and they are left to find their own way. Of course there are many twists and turns along the way that can delay, or upset even the best of plans, and this was certainly true in my case. The best advice I ever got from my father, and I say "best" because it came exactly when I most needed to hear it, was to never let expectations ruin your life. We all have dreams and goals, but sometimes reality gets in the way. The day-to-day struggles take priority and all too often years can slip by before we find a place in our minds (and souls) to be open to changes that allow these innermost dreams to come full cycle.

Once this happens, or I should say *if* and *when* it happens, you begin to understand what they call "the circle of life." So many things that occur along the way are truly less coincidental than we realize, and one day you begin to notice some small circles unexpectedly closing up, or more specifically, coming to fruition. Many others, however, are too big or convoluted to connect in any meaningful way within our own lifetime.

I should also clarify one other little point about my own experience: age is helpful.

I think many people have had unique experiences, or an interesting past worth sharing, but absolutely no idea where to begin. And others, perhaps, are simply not comfortable talking about themselves. Reading has always been such a big part of my life, like an old friend actually, so naturally I've always dreamed of publishing a book of my own someday. My goal throughout this memoir was to share some of the amazing and sometimes bizarre stories that have brought me to this moment in time without sounding too much like a "Dear diary."

I have an old friend who is an Episcopal priest, and one time while sharing a bottle of wine, the subject of art *versus* life came up. I mentioned how much I admired what he did, giving comfort and making a real difference in people's lives, compared to my work of making lawn ornaments.

He smiled and in a very gentle way corrected me on this point by sharing a story about his mother. She was undergoing regular cancer treatments that left her very sick, and absolutely dreaded each visit to the hospital.

There was a statue of the Holy Mother in one of the lobbies, and this was where she would start out. Placing a hand on the statue for a few minutes would calm her nerves and give her strength to get through it.

From that day forward I began doing the same thing, putting a hand on the tree before starting my work, and saying a small prayer while remembering that story.

Having said all that, somehow I've managed to scratch out a living for the past thirty-plus years by carving old tree stumps into something recognizable, and I attribute this to a little bit of talent, and a really lot of practice.

Now I take a moment to thank you, my reader, for taking time to read my little stories. This has turned out to be a bit more challenging than I first expected, but also a most enjoyable process and I sincerely hope that you found some enjoyment in it as well. I expect there may be some typos or rough spots, but just like a carving it's time to wrap it up here, Joe. I also hope this might inspire somebody else to start writing about some of their own personal life stories, it's never too late and I am living proof of that!

In closing, I'll just add one other quick note; a friend asked me one day if I could go back in time and change one thing in my life, what would it be? Silly question, but yes of course and here is the answer; I would have switched to Stihl chainsaws a lot sooner...

About the Author

Joe King has been a professional chainsaw artist for over thirty years and has worked in seven countries and over twenty-five states. He is a lifetime tree and wood enthusiast and still enjoys making furniture on occasion. In no particular order, other hobbies include traveling and photography, writing, playing guitar and harmonica with friends on occasion, and fixing up the garden, but mostly just spending time with friends and close ones. He has also been writing articles for various trade-related magazines for years and has been nationally published over fifty times. Joe has three sons and two grandchildren, and lives in the Laurel Highlands of Pennsylvania with his wife, Nelli. Plus a big crazy dog, and a mangy black cat.

I wish to thank a few people who helped bring this book, my dream, to fruition. Christie Moreton, my editor from the UK did such a great job sorting-out the big mess. Next is Sam "Fiverr" from Sri Lanka who made the cool cover design. Gary Skiff from Whidbey Island for the great photo of the bridge over Deception Pass.

For more information about this book, or my work in general, please visit my website;

www.treevarver.com

or

Chainsaw Chronicles @facebook.com